Philanthropy
in the Land of
the Gentleman
Millionaire

Begging For Alms With Dignity

by

Moussa Cissé

Translated by Roxane Christ

authorHOUSE™

1663 LIBERTY DRIVE, SUITE 200
BLOOMINGTON, INDIANA 47403
(800) 839-8640
WWW.AUTHORHOUSE.COM

First published by AuthorHouse 01/06/05

ISBN: 1-4208-0168-6 (sc)

Library of Congress Control Number: 2004097577

Printed in the United States of America
Bloomington, Indiana

This book is printed on acid-free paper.

Acknowledgements

My sincere thanks go to following persons and institutions for their invaluable contributions and assistance in the writing of this book.

The People
Mamadou Sylla – Community Resource Network
Oumar kaba – Community Resource Network
Diana Etindi – Consultant
Miniimah Cisse – Community Resource Network
Linda Bright – International African Community Council
Pamela Velo – The Indianapolis Foundation
Kamau Ziwanza – Rehab Resource, Inc
Safiatou Cisse – Toit Des Hommes
John Hall – Health and Hospital Corporation of Marion County
Ralph Dowes – Homeless Initiative Program
Tobby Miller – Greater Indianapolis Progress Committee
Aboubakary Keita – International African Community Council
Thomas Burn – Covering Kids Coalition, MCHD
Aboubacar Sidiki Sangare – International African Community Council
Boubacar Barry – International African Community Council
Stuart Sobel – Stuart Sobel Consulting, Inc

The Institutions
Center on Philanthropy at Indiana University
Central Indiana Community Foundation
Effroysom Funds
Greater Indianapolis Progress Committee
Homeless Initiative Program
Indianapolis Neighborhood Housing Partnership
Indianapolis Neighborhood Resource center
Nationality Council of Indianapolis
Rehab Resources, Inc
Stuart Sobel Consulting, Inc
The Fund Raising School
The Indianapolis Foundation
United Ways of Indiana

Table of Contents

Bibliography

Techniques and Principles of Fundraising, handbook, *The Center on Philanthropy at Indiana University, The Fund Raising School*

Interpersonal Communication for Fundraising handbook, *The Center on Philanthropy at Indiana University, The Fund Raising School*

Planned Giving: getting the Proper Start handbook, The *Center on Philanthropy at Indiana University, The Fund Raising School*

Developing Leadership for Major Gifts handbook, *The Center on Philanthropy at Indiana University, The Fund Raising School*

Grant Writing 101, Handbook, *Nonprofit Training Center, United Way of Central Indiana*

Indianapolis Neighborhood Leadership Academy, handbook, *Indianapolis Neighborhood Resource Center*

Starting your Neighborhood-Based Organization, *handbook, Indianapolis Neighborhood Resource Center*

Tax-exempt Status for Your Organization, *Publication 557, Internal Revenue Service, Rev. July 2001*

Instruction for Form 1023, *Internal Revenue Service, Rev. September 1998*

Non-Profit handbook, *National Edition*

National Center for Non Profit Board, handbook

Center for Nonprofit Training, handbook, *United Way of Central Indiana*

Sarah White, *Marketing Basics, alpha Books*

Scott M. Cutlip & Allen H. Center, *Effective Public Relations, 1982*

Joseph A. DeVito, *Message: Building Interpersonal Communication Skills, Addison Wesley Longman, 1999*

Bills R. Swetmon, *Communication Skills for The 21ˢᵗ Century, Skills-Epeak Press, 1998*

Introduction
Understanding the American Philanthropy
All from nothing

A well dressed man stopped a passer-by and asked him for a cigarette.

"Do you have a light?" retorted the latter. The first man felt his pockets in search of a lighter or even a match. In the end, he had to admit that he didn't have any means of lighting the cigarette on his person.

"Well, my brother," exclaimed the passer-by, "I'll have you know that I don't have a cigarette to give anyone if one doesn't have any means to light it."

The American philanthropist doesn't skimp over the means of assistance. But he doesn't give blindly. Such as the man who asked for the cigarette, a number of Non-Governmental Organizations (NGO) neglect to put in place the essential bases before making their way into soliciting funds from donors, be it locally or overseas. Any Non-Governmental Organization may evolve successfully regardless of their country of origin. In order to be successful the NGO will need to be established on the firm footing of: resources, education and community support. The United States abound in huge resources and charitable souls, all of them ready to put their hands in their pockets and help those in need. No one would question the fact that the countries of the Developing World are in desperate need of resources and education – which the United States have aplenty.

On one sunny morning, Mr. and Mrs. Leland Stanford showed up, without an appointment, at the office of the President of Harvard University in Boston. At first glance the couple could have passed for peasants who had no place in the prestigious learning institution, which is Harvard University. 'What do they want? They look like they've come from another era.' The secretary asked herself a little unnerved by the old people unwanted presence. The couple had requested an interview with the President of the University.

"The president will be busy all day; his diary his full." The secretary explained somewhat irritably.

"We'll wait," replied the old woman taking a seat beside her husband in the waiting room. The hours passed and the couple waited without showing any sign of impatience.

The secretary finally informed her boss of the couple's presence in the outer-office. "Maybe if you were to see them, they'll go away," suggested the lady who was quite annoyed by now.

The President relented and agreed to see the couple. Without preamble, he asked them what the point of their visit was. The old lady informed the President that her son had been a student at the university.

"He was very happy here. But he died in an accident a year ago. So my husband and I would like to erect a memorial for him somewhere in this campus."

"I am sorry," began the President, "but we cannot erect a statue in the memory of all those who have studied here and have since died. If we did, the place would resemble a cemetery."

"It's not a matter of erecting a statue," the old woman was quick to correct, "we were thinking of building a wing to the university in his memory…"

"Building a wing, did you say?" The president exclaimed a little taken aback. "Do you realize how much it cost to build a university wing? Well, what you have here is a patrimony of about eight millions dollars."

When she heard the figure mentioned by the president, the old lady bent down and whispered into her husband's ear: "If that's all it costs to start a university, why don't we build our own? I thought it would have been much more expensive than that."

A while after the interview, Mr. and Mrs. Stanford, went to Paolo Alto (CA) and founded the university that bares their name: The 'Leland Stanford University', in memory of their son, of whom Harvard University had no recollection.

Gentlemen Millionaires such as the Stanford couple, there are hundreds of thousands throughout the United States. The resources exist. They can come knocking at your door anytime, but they can very easily escape you if you don't know how to go grasp the opportunity. From the empire builders, movie stars and sports pros, singers, composers and other artists, to the inventors, executives and politicians – they all represent an opportunity that could come knocking.

To illustrate this fact, we will mention here some of the statistics which have been collected by the Center of Philanthropy at the University of Indiana regarding the Non-Governmental Organizations and their activities. More than 500 billion dollars are distributed annually by the non-profit organizations. There are approximately 56,000 private foundations with philanthropic vocation which support the NGO programs. There are millions of individual donors. Actually the individual donations surpass by far those of the foundations and of the other philanthropic institutions. They represent 75% of the total donated each year. The

NGO's employ directly more than 10 million people (or 1 in 15 people is employed by a NGO). There are over 850,000 non-profit organizations throughout the States. It is not surprising therefore, to note that the United States' philanthropy is by far the largest and the best organized in the world.

To the question whether the overseas organizations could have access to the immense resources and educational programs available through the philanthropic sector in the States, the answer is "yes" – at least theoretically. All of the organizations around the globe could benefit from the American Philanthropist's generosity, regardless of their country of origin. But in practice this is not as easy as it sounds. Today, such countries as Canada, Israel and Mexico, can qualify easily thought the IRS (Internal Revenue Services), to solicit directly charity funds from foundations, corporations, and residents of the United States. Nevertheless, the organizations established in other countries than those listed above, can also benefit from the American generosity. The proof of this is that the Bill Gates Foundation will grant 50 million dollars to private institutions throughout India in view of establishing new public health programs across the country.

All of this begs the question: "How can an organization benefit from the American charitable funds and resources?" A number of factors come into play when one needs to reach the hearts of generous donors. The most important of these is perhaps the one that deals with obtaining the IRS' blessing (Uncle' Sam's fiscal overseer). And believe me the American Philanthropist and Uncle Sam's IRS are no choir boys when it comes to monitor charitable activities.

Among the factors that come into play when entering the arena of American Charity, we will only investigate and review those which, in our view, are essential. We will review, in the next chapters, among many others, the following:

1. The freedom of association;
2. Mobilization of local resources;
3. How to communicate your ideas;

4. Education and Code of Ethics;
5. The financing sources;
6. Presentation of a financially viable project;
7. Constituents and transfer of know-how;
8. Lobbyism and Advocacy;
9. The planning of special events;
10. Leadership and the decision making process;
11. The Board of Directors;
12. The first legal document;
13. America and its four fundamental declarations;
14. The all important forms.

Now, let's go back to the elements which are necessary to the proper development of an organization: resources, education and community support. These three concepts are inseparable. Without resources there is no viable program. An organization can have all the resources possible at its disposal but without education of its leaders, it is vowed to fail. Resources and education would amount to nothing without the appropriate distribution of information and education of the constituents in view of obtaining support and active participation from the community.

Community Support

When the *International African Community Council* obtained subventions from two sources – the *Indianapolis Foundation* and the *Effroysom Fund* to establish a program of assistance to the African community in Indianapolis, in particular, and throughout the United States in general, hopes were very high. But the joy was short lived. In fact, the program was abandoned a little while later due to the lack of community support. As the President of this organization, I had to observe that the Africans who came to solicit funds from the organization, ironically, refused to register their presence. Why did they refuse? – "The organization would use their name to obtain subventions". As a result, the program, which was the first of its kind in the United States, had to shut its doors prematurely.

The concept of community support envelops interaction between organizations, population and public authorities. An organization can be in possession of all the resources available around the world, but if it doesn't have community support, its failure is guaranteed. Through this experience, I have learned that it is often more difficult for the NGO to obtain the cooperation and the support from the beneficiaries of their programs than that of the donors. Without community support, no organization will survive for very long. I have drawn two important lessons from this experience.

Firstly, there is a necessity to bring appropriate education to the NGO leaders. In the case of my experience with the International African Community Council, I had reached the conclusion that I was personally in need of a more in-depth formation addressing the management of an NGO. Therefore, at the closure of the program, I pursued my education in this area at the University of Indiana Center for Philanthropy and attending the Academic Leadership Program of Indianapolis.

Secondly, I came to realize that the African community had not been in receipt of the proper information regarding the nature of the program and the approach used by any NGO in the United States. So, education of the population and professional formation of the leaders in charge of the management of these organizations, are two of the basic elements aiming at the appropriate administration of financial and human resources. My experience at the head of the International African Community Council inspired me to write this book, which will relate the knowledge I have acquired in the domain of the management of an NGO in the United States, and which, I hope, will serve as a guide to others.

Resources without education; the key to failure
At the occasion of the fifth anniversary of the re-unification of Germany, a person from the old West Berlin remembered the extra personal expenses he had to incur and which had been provoked by the publicity that was aired through the television channels of West Berlin. "In fact," admitted the man, "my cousins who lived on the

other side of the wall had their televisions connected to the West Berlin channels and as soon as a new product would appear on the West Berlin market, I would receive a call from them the next day, and letters demanding that I sent them such and such item – things that I didn't even know existed on the market."

Today, it is a lot easier for the villagers lost in the confines of a poor country, to capture the signals from CNN, Canal Plus, and other stations – thanks to the satellite dishes, than it is for them to receive the signals from the TV stations in their own country. Such as in the case of the Berlin Wall, the waves have created glass walls; these walls expose the opulence of the rich countries to the eyes of the poor ones. They have invaded the lives of everyone even to the depth of the villagers' huts, hence creating massive immigration, brain drain and sometime civilization clashes.

The programs of some NGO's are partially or totally covered by public subventions. In addition to the humanitarian character of the subventions from the United States to the NGO's in the Developing Countries, there is also the 'self-preservation' of American interests in the Third World Countries when a subsidy is handed over. Very often, social troubles are provoked at the issue of the installation of western companies in any poor country, because the economic-improvement projects were not followed with socio-economic development programs beneficial to the community which hosted the western companies' projects in the first place.

Generally a government will negotiate investment projects in terms of number of employment created, taxes and levies which will be paid to the State where the project is established. And very often these taxes and employment opportunities have no direct impact on the lives of the thousands of citizens who live in the areas adjacent to the projects. In a number of cases, the government heads in charge of these projects, have never resided in the region were the project is located and have no relevant information concerning the area where an exploitation is to take place.

In 1992, the Australian company AREDOR, which was engaged in a diamond exploitation project near the county of Kerouane in Guinea, was attacked by the local population. The field work was stopped, the installations destroyed and the labs and offices burned to the ground. The army had to intervene and there were a number of deaths and several injured parties. As a journalist at that time; born in the area, the reporting I made of the crisis revealed that the most incisive claim from the local population had been the lack of spin-offs from the company into the socio-economic development of the area. There had been no concrete development program presented by the company to the local population. Everyone had assumed that either the company or the government was going to construct an infrastructure of schools, health centers and other facilities in the region – which never happened.

In fact, the contractual agreement passed between the Guinean government and the company called for levies to be remitted to the local community. But it was regrettable to observe that there had been no one designated to distribute the collected funds which were destined to the execution of the programs and which would have been all together beneficial to the population and to the company's reputation. It is also worthy of note that the Gold Exploration Company in Siguiri (not far from the Aredor fields) was subjected to similar troubles.

Another example – In Nigeria, the claims made by the Ogonis surrounding the oil exploitation of a certain company were also vindicated in blood. One of the most famous Ogonis' sons was executed at the issue of these events, even though the incident had created an international uproar at the time. These days, abductions, taking of hostages, occupation of petroleum production installations perpetrated by the local population have become common occurrences in Nigeria. The claims always surround the equitable distribution of resources. In most cases, there are funds available for the repartition to the local communities. But unfortunately, the local population is often neither informed nor educated to accede the resources available. In rare cases where the population is informed, it lacks the training to initiate the projects that would benefit the region. When the claims become virulent and threaten lives, the government has no other recourse than that of taking up arms to squash the population's unrest.

It is therefore clear, that without the education of the population and that of governments, resources solely, are not sufficient to bring prosperity and social stability to the community. In the cases cited above, among many others, we have demonstrated to a certain extent, that if the companies were to put in place the proper foundations for economic development (such as they do in their country of origin) and were to present the local population with financing programs which were adequately elaborated by properly structured NGO's, these companies would gain the sympathy of the local population – without question.

In view of the elements cited above, the American Non-Governmental Organizations are to be envied. Whilst the NGO's of the Third World countries have the devil by the tail, their American counterparts are doubly spoiled when it comes to available resources. Firstly, they enjoy the generosity of tens of thousands of philanthropists who donate millions of dollars every year; and secondly the United States fiscal code together with the tax relief allocated to the donors, encourage benevolence towards the American NGO's. On the other hand the formation programs offered to NGO members are of a very high educational level. And last but not least, the American population is thoroughly involved in projects of public interest.

In order to conquer the hearts of the American philanthropist, it is necessary to understand the American culture and the American mind set. These are at the origin of their incomparable generosity throughout the world. While paying a well deserved homage to the American spirit of generosity, it is however necessary to note that the genie of the philanthropy in the United States, to a large extent, owes its success to the fiscal facilities granted to the charitable organizations across the country. The fiscal code on taxes in its section 501(c)3 delineates the fiscal regime applicable to the various categories of charitable organizations which are tax-exempt. There are more than 30 types of non-profit organizations. *(See "Factor 1")*

To understand the spirit and the American philanthropic culture, it is necessary to take a look at the American settlement's origin on a land also called the "New World". When taking a closer look, I think that the dynamism of the philanthropy in the United States rests upon the emerging of new dynasties which are growing like mushrooms across the land. These dynasties have been founded by adventurers who, from practically nothing, found themselves in front of huge fortunes which surpass the natural needs of their families. All of that founded on the basis of the precept that America offers its citizens *freedom*; economic and political freedom, freedom of religion and of opinion, etc. The example of immigrants who have disembarked on the shores of the United States without a cent to their name and who are self-millionaires today, are to numerous to be counted. Carnegie, the king of steel, one of the pioneers of American philanthropy is one example among so many.

Contrary to the "Old Continent" where fortunes were built from ancestral generations, in America, with a little imagination and a lot of courage, citizens of modest means, have started from nothing to find themselves at the head of immense fortunes. From the long list of people who have thus 'arrived', we can mention Rockefeller (oil), Carnegie (steel), Lilly (pharmaceutical products), Bill Gates (software), etc. These men and women have a legendary reputation in the world of philanthropy.

One must understand that suffering and enduring misery are familiar and recent images etched in the minds of the one who has gone from nothing and has ended fortunate. Therefore, this person will be more inclined to understand human suffering and will be better disposed to help others. And this is at the apposite of the one who is born with a ready-made fortune (with a silver spoon in his mouth as it were) and for whom every thing is as it should be.

We can then conclude that the one, who has made his fortune alone, has a more liberal hand than the one who has inherited of his wealth. The heir of a fortune may not always be less sensitive to human suffering however, especially if the family patriarch has instituted a philanthropic culture among his heirs. Such is the case in the *Lilly Endowment*, where the foundation is managed by Ruth Lilly; heiress to Eli Lilly of Indianapolis. This foundation alone has a patrimony of more then twelve billion dollars dedicated to charitable organizations.

Apposite the builders, heirs may not have a liberal hand such as did his or her ancestor, because the patrimony is common to the family or institution established by the patriarch. On many occasions there is a need for several members of the family to agree on the distribution of funds available.

Most of industrial magnates in the States, made their fortune in other regions than those where they were born. The majority, in fact, are new comers to the community where they have made their fortune. Therefore most of them have no other links with the community than those of the employer – employee relations. So, all community donations emanating from the local industry are considered strictly as charitable donations. Again contrary to the Old Continent, where the barons of industry have been established in their community for centuries and where some families have served others for generations. The relations there, go beyond than that of employer to employees and thus the donations from the local industry are considered as normal gestures on the part of the barons.

In other words, in America, we are facing the 'Nouveau Riches', with new mentalities and new dynasties. This situation has contributed to some degree in giving the philanthropy in the United States an institutional dimension as opposed to other and older countries where charity is more or less of a personal nature. Charity in America has come out of the closet to become a highly professional, well structured and organized sector of activities governed by strict rules and regulations. Moreover any charitable activity is controlled by extremely rigid regulations imposed by the fiscal governing body (IRS) – this to avoid the risk of fraud.

The term 'Non-Governmental Organizations' should not be interpreted as describing entities, which would substitute any governmental institution, far from it; the NGO's constitute a complementary force to the government and to the business world, from which they withdraw their resources, either directly through subventions and donations or indirectly through the access to tax exonerations granted by the government.

In fact, there are not only the so called 'non-governmental' organizations, which according to the law and practice in force in the United States, benefit from tax-exonerated charitable donations. Public and private school institutions (elementary, secondary, university and other body of higher learning), hospitals, libraries, public and private museums are all great beneficiaries of charitable funds. The public institutions, at various levels, are at the origin of numerous non-profit organizations; their aim resides generally in the execution of social programs. As examples we can cite, among others; the *Great Indianapolis Progress Committee* and the *Indiana Neighborhood Housing Partnership*. They are organizations created by the Office of the Mayor of Indianapolis. Another example is the one of *SCORE* which is an organization that works closely with the *Small Business Administration* – a federal agency in charge of the management of small-to-medium size enterprises. SCORE employs retired (volunteers) who give some of their time to impart their relative expertise to assist small businesses in their development. This has entitled SCORE to become a privileged partner to the *Small Business Administration* agency. The programs elaborated and executed by several of these organizations are partially if not totally funded by the public purse.

When I was an employee at the *Wishard Memorial Hospital*, I was making a voluntary donation of $1.00 from each of my paychecks, or $26 per year. This contribution was automatically deducted from my salary and remitted to the United Way. The employees of many public and private services offer the same kind of voluntary contribution.

At a national level this represented several millions of dollars worth of contribution for this organization.

The case of the *United Way* is a flagrant example of the kind of support given by the American government to the NGO's. This organization has branches located in every community or collecting centers throughout the United States. The United Way and its branches collect funds from individuals, foundations, corporations and government agencies to support those programs engendered by community organizations which have limited funds for their development. Without the support provided by United Way, a number of community organizations would have a hard time collecting funds for their programs, because the competition is fierce. United Way benefits from government support at the highest level – up to the White House. Every President appears at least once a year in the public eye to give voice and support to this organization and its affiliates. However, United Way is not the only organization, which has been created under the government banner and which enjoys public support. Public subsidies are available to all organizations, either to execute programs initiated by the government or to engender their own programs.

The dynamism demonstrated by the NGO's in the United States has encouraged the authorities, the foundations, the corporations, and moreover the individuals to turn their regard towards the NGO's of the Third World and to making them worthy partners in view of the socio-economic development of the populations residing in 'the countries under development'. Almost all of the Aid Programs established in the Third World and which have been sanctioned by Congress, contain clauses detailing and enlisting the active participation of Non Governmental Organizations.

An old member of the American *Peace Corps* returned to a village in Africa where he had established a program aimed at ameliorating the preservation of local produce some ten years earlier. He was heart broken when he saw that the villagers were living in worse conditions than those in which they lived before the program had begun. This example is not isolated... Most of the programs, established by expatriates, disappear as soon as they leave. It is said that "You don't give for a cause; you give to someone with a cause". Therefore, it is up to the leaders of the Third World NGO's to adopt a professional attitude and to educate their constituents in order for them to have access to the American charitable resources which have no restriction other than ensuring that the funds allocated will serve to ameliorate the socio-economic conditions of the beneficiaries.

Factor 1
Freedom of Association
How to establish an organization in the
United States

There are three avenues leading to obtaining American charity. Firstly; establish a legitimate American organization and direct its operations towards the foreign country of one's choice. Secondly; register a NGO in a foreign country and attract the resources to that country. Thirdly; establish partnership relations with American NGO's, in order to benefit from their support.

NGO's in countries benefiting from fiscal exemptions

Today, the NGO's incorporated in countries such as Canada, Israel and Mexico enjoy the same privileges as their American counterparts. The NGO's in these countries can apply for tax-emption status directly to the Internal Revenue Services (IRS) – the United States federal taxation services.

What is a 'non-profit' organization?

Considered as non-profit organizations are those entities carrying one or more of the following activities:

1. Charity
2. Benevolence
3. Education
4. Civic
5. Patriotic
6. Politic
7. Religious
8. Social
9. Literary
10. Athletic
11. Scientific
12. Research
13. Agricultural
14. Horticultural
15. Soil improvement
16. Farming improvement
17. Improvement of domestic animal breeding
18. Professional, commercial, industrial, or association ecclesiastic
19. Promoting the development, establishment or expansion of Industry
20. Cooperatives, etc.

1. Establishment of a legitimate NGO

The establishment of a legitimate NGO in the United States demands the compliance to four legal formalities; the writing of the Articles of Constituency, the definition of the Articles of Incorporation; the acquisition of a federal employer's number and obtaining the letter defining the tax-exemption regime under which the organization will function.

A. The Articles of Constituency.

The Articles of Constituency is the first and most important legal document written by the members of an organization. It expresses in the form of 'minutes' taken during the 'First Organizational Meeting', the will of the signatories to constitute an entity of persons morally responsible in view of conducting activities common to all constituents.

The Articles generally comprise the following items:

- Date and venue of the meeting
- Name of people present and absent
- Name and purpose (objective or goal) of the organization
- Tax-exemption regime under which the organization will function.
- Nomination of the members of the Board of Directors comprising the President, the Secretary and the Treasurer of the organization as well as other directors.
- Nomination of the Declaring Agents
- The address of the organization.

(See sample in "Factor 12")

B. The Articles of Incorporation.

The Articles of Incorporation are delivered by the Secretary of State, in the State where the organization's head office is located. The establishment of NGO is prerogative to each State. Each State enforces laws and regulations in the matters of legislating and of the surveillance as to the proper functioning of an organization; whether they are qualified as non-profit or not. The incorporation of an organization is optional. However, an organization which is not incorporated will see its activities hindered in view of the fact that the incorporated organizations and institutions will distrust entities which do not have well defined judicial bases. The application for incorporation forms vary from State to State. These forms are available from the Secretary of State's office or on the Internet. The administrative or processing fees also vary from State to State.

The information to be provided in order to accede to the incorporation of an organization is generally the same; they comprise among other items:

- The name of the organization
- The address of the Principal Office

- The names, addresses and signature of the Incorporating Agents
- The purpose for the organization; the tax-exemption regime under which the organization will function; and a clause relative to the distribution of assets in case of dissolution of the organization.
- The category of membership (whether the organization will have members or not.)
- The names, addresses and signatures of the Registered Agents. The majority of States demands a minimum of three (3) incorporators

(See samples forms in "Factor 14")

C. Federal Employer's Number

The Federal Employer's Number is obtained on demand which should be addressed to the Bureau of Internal Revenue Services (IRS), the federal taxation service. Obtaining this number is mandatory and the responsibility of every corporation whether or not they are non-profit. There is no fee required to obtain this number. The form is known as the 'SS-4'. The information to be provided therein is:

- The name of the organization
- The address of the Principal Office
- Name, and address (street address only – PO Box will not be accepted) and Social Security number of the Declaring Agent.
- Incorporation date (which is not the same as the date when the Articles of Constituency were written).
- The purpose of the organization

(See sample forms in "Factor 14")

D. The letter defining the tax-exemption regime.

This letter is obtained on demand at the Bureau of Internal Revenue Services (IRS). The classification of the organizations which benefit from a tax-exemption regime is defined in Section 501(c) of the fiscal code. This classification comprises over 34 categories. However, the category number 501(c)3 is the one which, on top

4

of tax-exemption, offers advantages to the donors. The information contained in this book concern this particular category – it is the one that is of interest to us. *(See sample forms in "Factor 14")*

Organizations "501(c)3

The organizations said '501(c)3' are also called – 'Public Charity Organizations'. The tax-deductions linked with the donations made to this type of organizations have had their share of successes. In fact, the individuals, the corporations, the foundations which make donations to the 501(c)3 organizations all benefit from tax deductions.

The organizations susceptible to be classified in this category are organizations engaged in the following activities:

- Public Charity
- Religion
- Education
- Research
- Prevention against child cruelty and animal protection.

It is worth mentioning here that the final say remains with the IRS. Today the administration fees are in the order of $550.00

The information to be provided is onerous, complex and sensitive. It is suggested that a specialist be involved in this procedure. The form used to apply for tax-exemption is known as "Form 1023".

It is important to note that the examples given in this book are submitted only as an indication of what is required. In general, the law recommends to all applicants, when filling out the forms, to be assisted by a lawyer.

The Miranda Warning

It is worth remembering that in the United States "no one is supposed to know the law" – thereby the famous "Miranda Rule". It is in fact a variation of the basic interpretation of the Fifth Amendment to the Constitution which *proposes* that '…nor shall be compelled in any criminal case to be a witness against himself'.

Ernesto Miranda had been apprehended by the police for robbery. In the course of his interrogation, he ultimately confessed to a rape that happened a few days previously. We were in 1963. On the basis of his confession, Miranda was put on trial and found guilty of the crimes for which he was accused. His lawyer however, appealed the sentence by virtue of the fact that the police officers, at the time of Miranda's arrest, didn't advise him of his constitutional right which is at the basis of the Fifth Amendment. In 1966, the Supreme Court overturned the original decision and voted in favor of the plaintiff. Nevertheless, Miranda was found guilty of his misdeeds but this time not on the basis of his confession. Freed in 1973, after serving his sentence, Miranda was killed in 1976 at age of thirty-four when he was stabbed during an argument in a bar. Ironically, the police arrested a suspect who chose to remain silent after being read his "MIRANDA RIGHTS". The presumed assassin was released and no one was ever charged with the "Miranda" killing; simply because of the rights given under the Fifth Amendment. From that time onward, every Police Officer across the United States recites, to the alleged perpetrator of crimes, the formula known as the "Miranda Warning". This formula says that "You have the right to remain silent. However, everything you say during questioning can be used against you during your trial. You have the right to have counsel present during questioning. Should you be unable to afford a lawyer, one will be appointed for you".

2. Establishment of a NGO on American Soil.

A foreign NGO desirous to establish its organization on American Soil has to fulfill three principal requirements. First, it must register its establishment with the Secretary of State of one of the States in the Union. Second, it must obtain an 'Employer's Federal Number' and third, it must obtain a letter from the IRS defining the tax-exemption regime under which it will function.

A. Register a foreign organization.

The organization must find the person who will be its representative (or agent) on American Soil. This person has to be a resident of the United States and residing in the State where the organization wishes to conduct its activities.

What is a Foreign NGO?

In this book, the term 'Foreign NGO' is used to designate any and all non-profit organizations incorporated in a country other than in one of the States of the United States. In fact, the term 'Foreign Organization' could lead to confusion in the mind of a layman, because according the United States' Constitution, the regulation concerning the establishment and the incorporation of a *foreign* organization in any State of the Union is governed by the *State* in which the organization is intending to conduct its activities and is not governed by the Federal Government. Therefore, the laws of each of the States define an organization as 'foreign' an organization not yet established in their State. For example, the government of the State of Indiana will consider as 'foreign' any NGO incorporated in the Republic of Guinea, in France, in Japan, in China or in Canada as well as an organization incorporated in the State of Illinois, or in Texas, etc. It is a reciprocal rule adopted by all the States in the Union.

B. Obtaining an 'Employer's Federal Number'.

The process has been described in the previous paragraphs.

C. Obtaining the letter defining the tax-exemption regime.

The process has been described in the previous paragraphs.

3. Establishing partnership relations.

Establishing partnership relations with an American organization does not necessitate the compliance to any formality other than that required by the American partner. However, it is important to underline here that such partnership must be established on solid bases, sealed with such documents as agreements, contracts, memorandum of understanding, etc. In this regard, and once again, it is suggested to seek the assistance of legal counsel to ratify these documents and never to assume anything that is not written in these documents. Taking legal actions is one of America's favorite sports. The only thing that one could assume is that any document signed by an American, one of these days, will find its way in front of a judge. This I mention without prejudice.

Abraham Lincoln, President of the United States between 1861 and 1865, liked to tell the story of one his clients at the time he was practicing law. His client had a hard time recovering the two dollars that someone owed him. He asked Lincoln to assist him in recovering his money. Lincoln attempted to convince the client of the little he had to gain by engaging in legal proceedings – to no avail. Lincoln then asks the client to give him a provision of five dollars to defend the case. With the five dollars, Lincoln gave two dollars to the defendant in the case; who in turn reimbursed the client and kept the three dollars as his fee. The case was thus resolved to the benefit of all concerned.

It is essential for an American that justice be done. For him justice has no price. We will come back to that subject later.

4. Classification of the tax-exempt organizations.

In fact, the Internal Revenue Code of the Internal Revenue Service (IRS) defines, under its Section 501(c), the different categories of organizations subject to tax exonerations. There are over 34 categories of organizations which are classified according to their sector of activities.

The organizations classified under Section 501(c)3 are particularly unique inasmuch as the funds donated to these organizations are said to be 'tax-deductible' on the donor's part.

The other categories described in Section 501(c) have their revenue exonerated of taxes. But the donor's contributions are not 'tax-deductible'.

The listing below is a summary presentation of the document in the hands of the IRS. You must consult a specialist to determine the regime which will be better applicable to your particular organization. But one must make note that the final decision rests with the IRS as to the classification category applicable to your organization.

The difficulty to find a generic name describing each type of organizations has led the IRS to using 'numbers' instead of names to define each category comprised in the classification.

501(c)1: Corporations Organized under Act of the American Congress.

501(c)2: Title-Holding corporations for tax-exempt organizations.

501(c)3: Organizations described as charitable, religious, educational, scientific, literary; or organized in the domain of the prevention of cruelty against children and of the animal protection. *These organizations are said to be of 'Public Charity' because they generally draw their funds from 'public' donation.*

501(c)4: Organizations of civic leagues, social welfare and comprising local associations of employees.

501(c)5: Labor, Agricultural and Horticultural organizations,

501(c)6: Business Leagues, Chamber of Commerce, Real Estate Board.

501(c)7: Social and recreational Club /organizations.

501(c)8: Fraternity Associations or organizations from which the 'lodges' pay compensations to their members for death in the family, sickness, accidents or other benefits.

501(c)9: Voluntary Association of employees designed to pay part of the company's profits to their members for death in the family, sickness, accidents, or other benefits.

501(c)10: Domestic Fraternal Societies and associations from which the 'lodges' assign their net revenue to their members' charitable causes, fraternity, and specific causes which *do not* include death in the family, sickness, accidents.

501(c)11: Teachers' Retirement Funds Associations established for the sole purpose of distributing their revenue to their members in the form of a pension.

501(c)12: Benevolent Life Insurance Associations designed to pay life insurance benefits to their members. And, associations which provide funds for the construction and maintenance of irrigation systems across farmland, or telephone company 'cooperatives' which are designated and provide essential services to the community at large.

501(c)13: Cemetery companies.

501(c)14: Credit Unions created under the banner of the States and other organizations designed for the maintenance and appropriate distribution (or lending) of funds to their members.

501(c)15: Mutual Insurance Companies which provide their members with insurances at considerably reduced costs.

501(c)16: Organizations and Cooperatives which finance crop operations in connections with the marketing and the purchase of agricultural produce by the organization.

501(c)17: Supplemental Unemployment Benefits Trust organizations which pay supplemental benefits to their members who are out of work.

501(c)18: Employee-Funded Pension Trust created by employees' organizations (founded prior to 25th June 1959) which effect payment of pensions to their members from the funds saved by the employees during the term of their employment.

501(c)19: Post or Organizations of past or Present members of the armed forces.

501(c)21: Black Lung Benefit Trusts, which, as its name implies, is designed to pay compensations to members who have contracted 'Black Lung' disease whilst working in the coal mines across the States. *These organizations were founded by the coal mine owners and operators in view of fulfilling their responsibilities towards their employees when they are suffering from the disease or succumb from it.*

501(c)22: Withdrawal Liability Payment Funds. These organizations provide funds to meet the liability of employer withdrawing from a multi-employer pension fund.

501(c)23: Veterans' Organizations (founded prior 1880) designed to provide the veterans' of wars with insurances and other ensuing benefits.

501(c)25: Title-Holding corporations or Trust with multiple parents. Companies designed for the sole purpose of ensuring the safe-keeping of trusts established by organizations, corporations, or companies having multiple 'parent companies' at their helm. These consignment companies distribute the revenue collected from their properties to 35 (or less) parents or beneficiaries.

501(c)26: Organizations sponsored by the States to provide medical coverage to those people suffering from 'high risk' diseases or malady.

501(c)27: Organizations sponsored by the States designed to ensure the re-insurability of their workers.

501(d): Religious and apostolic Organizations.

501(e): Hospital and Services cooperatives, which provide service fees to their members.

501(f): Organizations servicing the 'Educational Operations' cooperatives or organizations. They provide collective investment services to members of the Education Profession.

501(k): Child Care Organizations serving and surveying the operations of daycare centers and other children benefit organizations.

501(n): Charitable Risk Pools which insure their members against the risks to funding or donating to organizations classified under Section 501(c)3.

521(a)1: Farmers' Cooperatives Associations. Cooperatives designed for the marketing and the purchase of agricultural products.

527: Political Organizations. The parties, committees, funds, associations, etc., which are directly or indirectly accepting contributions or have expenditures related to political campaigns.

5. The three principal types of organizations.
There are three principal types of organizations:

1. The Charitable or 'Public Benefit' Organization;
2. The Religious Organization;
3. The Organizations said to be to the 'mutual benefit' of its members.

You need to choose one of these types at the time you need to incorporate your organization.

- **Charitable or Public Benefit Organizations.** These organizations are commonly called 'Public Charity' Organizations and are classified in the category 501(c)3.
- **Religious Organizations.** This group comprises organizations dedicated to the management of devotion sites, such as churches, mosques, synagogues, temples, etc. They also comprise organizations dedicated to the propagation of faith or ministry such as evangelization through the media channels or conferences, seminars or religious activities other than those regularly practiced at the site of devotions. Lastly the group enlists various religious organizations or Samaritan organizations which are distributing their funds to social causes. These organizations are also classified in the category 501(c)3.

- **'Mutual Benefit' Organizations** – Also referred to as 'Professional organizations, Fraternity organizations, Cooperatives, or Syndicates, etc. These are classified in one or the other sections of the Taxation Code.

6. The naming of an organization.

It is important to give some pointers regarding the naming of an organization.

Double use of names – The laws of the States will only protect the names of organizations that have been incorporated under their jurisdiction. This protection is only applicable within the boundaries of each of the States. Anyone can use the name of your organization in another State without violating any laws of the State where your organization is registered. Therefore, in order to protect the name of your organization at Federal level, it will be necessary to have it registered with the Federal Bureau of Trade's Marks.

The language chosen for the name of your organization – There is no restriction as to the choice of language. However, the name should be written in Latin alphabet.

The translation of your organization's name is not exclusive – The translation of the name of your organization is not exclusive property of your organizations, unless you register the name in the language(s) used in the translation. If a foreign NGO wishes to do business in America under a name that has been translated from its original language, this organization needs to ensure that the English version of its name is not already in use by a local organization. For example; let's suppose that the French organization "Médecins Sans Frontières" wishes to extend its activities in the United States under the English version of its name – "Doctors without Borders". That organization could not be registered under that English version of its name because of another organization being already registered at the federal level under the same name.

Please note; that any resemblance with existing situations is purely coincidental.

Easily identifiable terminology – If your organization has 'international' ambitions, choose a name that is easily identifiable by the public the world over. Example; 'Center', 'Association', 'Action', 'International', 'Programs', 'Project', etc.

Confusing terminology – Avoid using confusing terminology; example – 'Union', in the United States this appellation is reserved to syndicates. If your organization is not a 'syndicate' or a 'union' per se, using a name comprising these words would lead to confusion.

"Association" usually designates organizations formed for the 'mutual benefit' of their members. These 'professional', 'fraternity' types of associations are *not* considered as 'Public Charity' organizations, unless the members are themselves organizations classified under Section 501(c)3 of the Tax Code. These 'Association' do not benefit from 'tax-deductible' donations.

Proper choice: Example; Association of French Journalists – a professional association; The Women's Association – an association the members of which are themselves organizations.

Improper choice: The use of the term 'association' could discourage the participation of key members of society. Example; "Association of the <u>Natives</u> of Kerouane" – you're immediately and definitely closing the door on anyone who is not a 'native' of Kerouane.

Names referring to continents, country or cities

As much as possible, avoid referring to a continent, a country, or to a city when choosing the name of your organization. The names using such reference could deter good will minded people who would be useful as members or donors of your organization. On the other hand such name could attract the attendance of people natives of the place cited in the name and who could have malevolent intentions or engender destructive actions towards your organization.

Improper choice: "Association of the Natives of Kerouane for the fight against drought."

Proper choice: "Action against Drought."

Proper usage: - We have to keep in mind that the suggestions made in this book are essentially aimed at those organizations which are created in view of gaining the American public support towards programs of public interest established in foreign countries. We are calling 'American public support', any and all donations made by individuals, foundations, corporations and from time to time, governmental offices, to an organizations classified in the category 501(c)3. Therefore, what was said above does not encompass the organizations that have been created for the sole purpose of re-grouping people of one nation, city or continent in view of re-creating a cultural environment or promoting the maintenance of a culture or historic values. This type of organizations is due to use the continent, country or city in the name they have chosen; example; 'Center for Cultural Development in Guinea.'

Mileage Name: - Its name is the first marketing tool of an organization; it has to be short, concise and meaningful. The name has to state in a very few words the object (or goal) of the organization. Using only two or three words would be ideal, such as 'Red Cross', 'Doctors without Borders', 'Reporters without Borders', 'Habitat for Humanity', etc. This rule is not applicable when it comes to the professional organizations which must be explicit when it comes to qualifying its membership. Usually these organizations operate under an acronym – example; 'American Association of Petroleum Geologists', which function under the acronym of AAPG. These organizations exist for their members only and for those who recognize the acronym or 'mileage name' and wish to participate in their activities. However, when it comes to the 'Public Charity' organizations, they exist for the public and by the public. Therefore they need to identify their aim (or goal) into their name.

Use of acronyms: - As we have pointed out previously, if the use of acronym is acceptable (or even recommended) when it comes to the name of a 'professional' organization, it is not so for a NGO geared to obtain Public Charity contributions. Therefore, a public charity organization should avoid the use of an acronym when choosing a name; this for the simple reason that you would not be recognized readily by a person (or another organization) interested in your goal or activities. 'Habitat for Humanity' brings much better results than 'HFH' would!

A name that means everything to everyone: - You should avoid choosing a name that 'means everything to everyone'. The donors distrust the organizations that embrace more than one subject or of which the name leads to something else... The improper choice in this case would be the one of a community organization that implies to be at the stem of *the* development of its city or even of its country. For example the 'Association for the socio-economic development of Nulpareh' does not define clearly which sector of 'socio-economic development' the association intends to address. The donor would be tempted to imagine that the funds allocated to such an organization could be dedicated to the *educational* development of the community, when in fact the funds could be dedicated to the improvement *fishing methods* used in the area or to infrastructure development, or other. Therefore, if the village of Nulpareh needs socio-economic development funds addressing a variety of projects, the community needs to establish distinct and separate organizations for each sector to which the funds will be allocated – for example 'Action for Agricultural Development' or 'Action for environmental improvement' or 'Action for health care establishment' etc. These organizations could therefore, go in close-ranks towards the donors presenting them with precise and well-defined programs which would be complementing one another and would retain the attention of many more donors as well. The donors would then know who does what, when and where. Moreover this method allows each organization to express their requests according to their field of knowledge and their respective responsibility. Not to mention that in so doing one avoids leadership conflicts which are the principal cause of an organization's demise.

Factor 2
Mobilization of Local Resources
Power to attract external resources

'If you don't believe in what you are doing no one else will.' The story of Mr. M.C. Thomas illustrates this idiom.

Mr. M.C. Thomas went before the judge accused of the murder of his wife, although there was no tangible evidence that his wife was in fact dead since her body had not been recovered. And since, it is well known in legal terms that if there isn't a body, there isn't a crime, Mr. Thomas shouldn't have been in court in the first place. Nevertheless the prosecutor thought that there was enough damaging evidence against Mr. Thomas to convince the twelve members of the jury of his guilt. In his closing statement, the defense counsel asserted, when he addressed the jury, that his client was innocent. In evidence of that, he maintained that the victim was standing behind the door, and that she was due to appear in court at any moment. Everyone in the audience, including the members of the jury, turned their head in the direction of the door. Outwardly ignoring the public's reaction the defense lawyer pursued his argument on the basis of 'no body thus no crime'. He concluded his statement saying to the members of the jury that they were about to commit a grave error if they were to find his client guilty – "Because," said he, "you are not convinced that Mrs. Thomas is dead. When I told you that the alleged victim was standing behind the door ready to make an appearance; every one of you turned your gaze towards the door. If you had *absolutely* no doubt that Mrs. Thomas was dead, you wouldn't have turned your eyes to the door."

At the conclusion of their deliberation, the jury returned to court and presented a verdict of "*guilty as charged*" to the presiding judge! The defense counsel couldn't believe his ears. Confident that he had convinced the jury of his client's innocence, he was positively puzzled by this turn of event. Thus he approached one of the members of the jury and asked if he could enlighten him as to the reason for their surprising decision. The latter replied that yes, the jurors had some doubts as to the culpability of his client, but all doubts had been set aside when the jurors had observed the attitude of the accused at one crucial moment – "When you announced that Mrs. Thomas was standing behind the door and waiting to appear in court everyone turned their head towards the door *except for your client* who didn't move a muscle! He knew that his wife was dead and that she could never come through the door."

As we've mentioned previously, if you don't believe in what you're doing no one will. Therefore, you cannot convince anyone to participate into your programs or projects if you don't believe they're worthwhile in the first place, or if you don't take the first step to ascertain that they are in fact *worthwhile* in *your* eyes.

According to several studies on the subject, the community groups living in Third World countries have a very particular and high philanthropic culture. However, these groups intervene in a very informal manner which addresses mostly the problems related to families, nearby environment or neighborhood. They do this without any formal framework while leaving no trace of their passage and no record of their efforts. Without evidence to show the impact or progress made by these community groups, the would-be sponsor would have a difficult time to assess the needs and propose assistance. It is necessary to remember that 'one doesn't give *to a cause* but *to a man with a cause'*. The best way to attract foreign resources into Third World countries is to create a framework which can host external resources such as the 'Foundations' can. The reports from these communities and institutions would provide an excellent data base of information concerning a region in need of assistance and could also provide a solid relay basis of control for the American Foundations desirous to offer assistance in foreign soil.

Elements affecting the motivation of American Donors

As we have indicated in the previous paragraphs it is necessary to complement any 'education' with the establishment of structures, institutions and financial mechanisms, which will form the basis and the framework of credible interventions in the eyes of the NGO in the United States. These organizations should be similar and conforming to their would-be American partners when it comes to their financial mechanisms or to their internal operations. Such structures, best known in the States are:

- Private Foundation
- Corporate Foundation
- Community Foundation
- Community Center
- Resource Centers for community based organizations
- Government Funds destined to NGO support
- Special Events Support Organizations.

The Stereotypes

Certain countries of the Third World are victims of 'stereotyping'. This is due to the manner in which the press and other media fiends seeking the sensational, report on what's happening in Africa and elsewhere.

Adapt to the 'local colors'

Soon after my arrival in the United States, I was under the false impression that everyone admired my 'grand-boubou' embroidered gowns. Finally I realized that every time I was wearing such a gown and went to an office; the steps I was trying to take and my enquiries were always in vain or met with cold shoulders. And, I

soon understood that the manner in which I dressed was at fault
– when I wore a suit like everyone else did, my affairs were easily
concluded. Not everyone approves of *the strangers* in their country.
In my case, the 'grand-boubou' allowed my interlocutors to evaluate
if the *stranger* in front of them had the right to have access to such
or such services. All this was done in good faith mind you – but I
changed my dress-code and my tactics; and it works!

For your meetings with your American partners, don't try to
impress them with your traditional dress. You would probably be the
subject of unwarranted ridicule and it would have a nasty effect on
the result of your meeting. This is because Americans are very quick
to associate the manner in which you dress with the primitiveness of
your background – as reported in the media; which will put in doubt
everything you're trying to accomplish.

Words that could turn against you

If there is any doubt as to your management capacity, it goes
without saying that no one will entrust you with consequential
projects. Always introduce your project in the best way possible.
Present your achievements, if need be, those of your partners and
those of your competitors. (It is always best to keep your friend
close-by and your enemies even closer!) You must avoid putting the
government, public authorities of your country or your competitors
in a bad light. If you can't say anything good about someone don't
say anything. To show the incompetence of a government will put
doubts in the minds of the donors regarding *your own* honesty. But
first and foremost, the donors will want the assurance that if he
allocates funds to your organization, he is insured that justice be
done in case of disagreement or misappropriation – he wants to be
able to turn to the government and to seeing justice done (if such is
the need).

If you show that your would-be sponsor cannot count on law and
order in your country he will think twice before putting a penny down.
And if it is of public knowledge that your country's government
suffers from corruption don't dig your hole any deeper... In the

eyes of the sponsor, the men at the head of your country or the ones managing your organization were made in the same mold. Therefore by showing your competitors or your country's government under a *dim* light, you're inviting to direct a *strobe* light on yourself – their findings could be catastrophic for everyone concerned.

It is also suggested not to demonstrate political tendencies one way or the other. If the donors, or local authorities have not the same political beliefs than you do, leave it alone – again every one would lose in case of conflicting political views being exposed to scrutiny.

Factor 3
Knowing how to communicate your ideas
Information is power

During a conversation, between the former Security Minister of Guinea, Dr. Koureissy Conde, and the former South African President, Nelson Mandela, Dr. Conde complimented the 'freedom fighter' on his outward attitude of never being afraid of anything. To this compliment, Mr. Mandela didn't omit to remark that nevertheless he was afraid of one thing – "the danger represented by the services of an interpreter."

We are only transmitting messages in words, in gestures which are interpreted by our interlocutors and which make sense in their minds. If your messages are wrongly interpreted or badly perceived, they could be prejudicial to your cause. Communicating is based on the interpretation and on the sense that your audience will give to your messages expressed in words, attitudes, gestures, body language, etc. You must not think that the interpretation resides only in the translation of the words from one language to another. It resides mainly in the manner in which these messages are received (or perceived) by the audience. One could say that words don't find their true meaning in a dictionary. The meaning of your words is found however, in the interpretation the audience gives to your messages. If we don't transmit the meaning of the words, we are only transmitting messages which are subject to erroneous interpretations. This is why in journalistic terms, when someone tells you that 'it was not what I meant to say'; nine times out of ten you can be sure that it was 'exactly what the person meant to say'!

Definition: In simple terms 'communication' is the ensemble of means used in the emission, the reception, the decoding and the interpretation of any spoken or written message.

Some sensitive points about 'communicating'

- **Don't worry about speaking clearly – worry about being clearly understood.** Ask yourself this question: "How will I transmit this message so that it would not be subject to the wrong interpretation?"
- **Communication techniques are acquired not innate.** At birth, you could only cry or scream and not speak. We learn to speak by imitating others. This process is actually endless.
- **Assume that your next message will not be understood.** Always communicate intelligently; pay attention to the feedback and blame only yourself when you receive a negative result.
- **The sense given to your words comes from the way you have expressed your message rather than from the words themselves.** In fact 90% of the sense given to your message is attributed to your tone of voice, your attitude and your body language rather than to the words contained in your message.
- **Every time two people face each other; they're communicating.** Even though you may not utter a word, be aware that you are transmitting a message. In such condition, you could transmit the wrong message which may not be well received. Beware: "you can't avoid to communicating."

- **Eighty-five percent of the information stocked in the human mind has entered it through the eyes.** When your words are in conflict with your attitude (or your body language), your listener will interpret your message based on what *he saw* in your attitude.
- **Communication is a complex process; continuous, dynamic and ever changing.** Contrary to what people may think, simply exchanging words is not sufficient to be understood. Many things could affect or alter the way you communicate.

The Language

Language: When the Chinese decided to introduce the teaching of languages in schools, they discovered, after studying the impact this decision would have on the 'people', that due to the ever increasing Chinese population across the world, in three hundred years four out of five people will be Chinese. Therefore, the powers that be decided that it was *not necessary* for the Chinese People to learn another language. I don't know if the Americans have reached the same conclusion! However, what is certain is that the learning of a foreign language is not an American forte. So it is absolutely vital to learn the rudiments of the English language – by courtesy. It is also necessary to have all your essential documentation translated in English; because you will rarely find an American who speaks another language than English. If you cannot learn English – for whatever reason, the services of an interpreter will be necessary.

- Avoid using jargons
- Learn the terminology
- Ensure that your interpreter uses the proper terminology
- Be concise and precise in the formulation of your correspondence or proposal.
- There is no one lazier than an interpreter! They will translate in two words what took you twenty to express in a phrase.
- Don't assume that the expressions which are 'usual' in your culture are such in the American culture.
- Control your body language.

Non-verbal language – Are the messages we are transmitting through our body language, our gestures, our movements, our stance, etc.

Contradictory message – Body language could contradict the spoken word. When you visit someone in hospital; it is his grimacing face that will tell you in how much pain he is, although his words may be dismissing the fact or evading the subject.

Offensive attitudes – Certain attitudes are offensive depending on the surroundings and your cultural heritage. For example snapping your fingers to attract someone's attention is offensive to an American. In certain culture, looking at a person in high places straight in the eyes is a sign of disrespect – in America, the opposite is true.

Dress, Décor and punctuality

The way you dress, the décor surrounding your meetings and the respect for punctuality are all forms of expression which communicate a particular message to your interlocutors.

Dress code – Knowing how to dress given the occasion is important; try to 'dress for the circumstances' as it were – marriages, dinner, funeral, reception, etc. On the other hand always inform your guest of the required dress-code; be it casual, formal, black-tie, etc. We have mentioned previously the inconvenience of wearing traditional outfits in particular circumstances – (See 'Factor 2') it is therefore important to take into account the impact the way you dress will have on the people you meet. Wearing traditional garments is better recommended when attending a cultural reunion or festivity and not recommended when attending a business meeting.

Décor – Decorate the venue of any meeting adequately and appropriately. Put in place objects around the room and pin posters on the walls that communicate a message responding to the circumstances. On May 1st 2003, the American President, George Bush at the commands of military jet, landed on an aircraft carrier in order to give a speech to the troops regarding the development of the Iraqi war. On a banner stretched across the podium, inscribed in very large letters, one could read the following words: "MISSION ACCOMPLISHED" – when in fact the *mission* in Iraq was *far from being accomplished* at that time. The President's political adversaries were very quick to accuse him of 'declaring the end to the hostilities' before time. However, that message on the banner is what the world *saw* and *understood* from the President's public address on that day – although those words were never pronounced.

Punctuality – Be punctual, respect the appointed time; don't be late, and don't be too early for an appointment – walking in five or ten minutes in advance is adequate timing. Never arrive thirty or even an hour in advance unless it is necessary for you to complete some other formalities prior to a meeting. When you arrive too early for a meeting it generally means that you have nothing else to do. On the other hand, being late fifteen minutes for a meeting is acceptable. But if you have to be late at all, take care to phone and advise your partner that such will be the case. If you cannot attend a meeting at all; don't wait for the last minute to inform all parties concerned of your intended absence.

The NGO's desirous to access American Charity need to learn how to impart their messages. This necessitates the elaboration of an appropriate plan of communication. In order to do so, you need to be aware of the different channels, techniques and vehicles of communication in use in the United States. One cannot speak of communication without mentioning the word 'media'. The media is the vehicle which provides for the transmission of your messages. To transmit a message through the media channels such as the 'press' you have two choices. First you can pay for your advertising space; or you need to create an event of interest to the journalist. However, it is not a fact that all events warranting a press report will consequently be a report in favor of your organization. Journalists define as 'news' or 'newsworthy' every item that is published in a newspaper. In other words, it's the journalist who decides what is 'news' and what is not.

The six items of considerations – which will make the 'news'

It is therefore important for the NGO leaders to be aware of the six principal items that will determine, in the eyes of a journalist, whether or not an event is 'worthy' to be reported in their newspaper. For an event to have a journalistic value (or be 'newsworthy') in the eyes of the press, it must be respond to one or more of the six following considerations:

1. Redaction value
2. Notoriety
3. Proximity
4. Conflict
5. Opportunity, and
6. The unconventional or be a matter of 'curiosity'.

Thus, when an event contains one or more of these six elements it is deemed to have journalistic value or 'be newsworthy'.

Redaction value – To have redaction value an event must support the opinion, the culture or the philosophy of the press establishment. "Freedom of Press" or not, redaction value is by far the determining factor when treating of an event in the press. The redaction value is based on economic, political, moral, and philosophical readership trends.

The mini-series on the former President Ronald Reagan, produced by an American television broadcaster, provoked a general uproar in the conservative camp of American politics. These politicians deemed the former president's representation without basis and impartial. CBS was forced to cancel the program afraid that the show would be boycotted from the advertisers.

In truth, the press' economic interest weighs heavily on the scale of treatment of any information. Every press organism adopt a line of 'redaction value' commensurate with the readership it addresses. The advertisers buy publicity space in the organisms susceptible to transmit their messages to the population they have targeted. The preservation of, political, moral, philosophic or cultural values, is aimed at protecting the economic interest of the targeted readership (or audience). The Donahue Show was cancelled on MSNBC because the majority of Donahue's guests were anti-war at a time when the Iraqi war (2003) sold well on the small screen. MSNBC could see the ratings of its rival FOX NEWS climbing the charts because of the latter's radical position in favor of the Iraqi war.

When you need to send a message through the media make sure that you choose the organism that defends similar values to yours.

Notoriety – The 'newsworthy' item, one way or another, will see political figures (presidents, ministers, senators), renown artists of the cinema, television, or sports' celebrities involved in the event. Michael Jackson being accused of child molestation was sufficient for the media around the world to grab hold of this event and make it immediately 'newsworthy'. Meanwhile, there are thousands of child molestation cases across the United States every day that will go unreported and will never 'make the news'.

Solicit the support of a celebrity to support your programs when you need the press to turn their attention to your organization.

Proximity – This kind of event has an impact on the readership or the audience. The public is interested in the events that occur in close proximity of their residence (neighborhood, city, region, country, etc.). The press will deal with events that have a direct impact on the audience or readers in their immediate vicinity. The press, in particular, has a very short geographic radius of readership.

Therefore, choose a press organism which is in close proximity to the beneficiaries of your programs.

Conflict - Conflict is at the basis of the human being' success; man revels in conflicts of all kinds. Any form of adversity between two or more men or between men and nature such as wars, political debates, elections and even competitive sports or other artistic or cultural competitions will be classified as conflicts. All of those events are abundantly covered by the press or media.

Avoid the conflict type of events which could be prejudicial to your cause; but organize events based on 'conflicts' such as sport, cultural or artistic competitions which can show your organization under a profitable angle.

Opportunity – The event must give the opportunity to talk about another fact. When OJ Simpson, accused of the murder of his wife, was pursued by the police through the streets of Los Angeles, he was at the wheel of a "BRONCO". During the chase all the television programs were interrupted to follow the chase on the screen. The audience remembered one thing; the BRONCO's performance. In the days that followed, the sales of the 4X4 BRONCO were unprecedented in the history of that vehicle. This free publicity made under very unfortunate circumstances qualifies as an 'opportunity'. It resulted in sales equaling millions of dollars which the regular publicity could never have hoped to attain.

Don't miss an opportunity which could land you with article in the press related to your organization. In the world of publicity it is said that 'any publicity is good publicity'.

The opportunities often present themselves in the form of events that the journalists call 'false events'. These are events which are created to commemorate or recall a 'real event' that has occurred in the past. In this category you will find the anniversaries of the death of historic figures, or commemoration of an historic event such as 'Independence Day, Centennial Day, etc. The events such as fairs, carnivals, expositions, seminars, conferences, are also classified under this category.

Unconventional or 'curious' item – This is classified as an extraordinary event. It is said that 'when a dog bites a man it is not newsworthy; but when a man bites a dog – that's news!

Communication

The communication channels

Those are the paths through which a message is transmitted to an audience. In marketing, we are referring to communications as the means by which promotional information are transmitted to the targeted population. Communication channels can either be 'interpersonal' or 'non-personal'.

Interpersonal communication – The interpersonal communication means that two or more people communicate among themselves. (Face to face, telemarketing, public speeches or personalized correspondence).

Non-personal communication – The non-personal communication transmits the message using means that do not necessitate personal contact or interaction between the person sending the message and the audience. (Radio, television, newspaper, pamphlets, films, etc.) Non-personal communication can be attained using written or mechanic means.

- **Written means of communication** – is defined as any form of communications transmitting a message via conventional written, designed words or images such as letters, posters, drawings, signs, etc.
- **Mechanical means of communication** – describes any mechanical means used to store a message (written or spoken) and which can be re-transmitted at a later date to any audience of choice – those comprise floppy discs, CD's, tapes, DVD's, films, slides, Internet, etc.

Information

We are inundated every day by an ocean of information that has been stored (and released) in four distinct formats:

1. Printed
2. Film
3. Magnetic – CD Rom, magnetic tapes, VCR tapes etc.

4. Optical – CD, DVD, etc.

More than 90% of the news is stored on magnetic formats with only 7% stored on film and the last 3% being stored on printed or optical media.

Advertisement

A wise man said: "to avoid paying for the advertising your product in hopes to save money; is like stopping your clock in hopes to save time." Today any organization is forced to use various means of advertisement to inform the public of the existence of its programs.

Publicity is the echo the media transmit to the public regarding your organization free of charge; different from Advertisement which is paid.

Advertisement has three (3) aims:

1. Inform the public of the existence of a program, product, service or organization.
2. Persuade the public of the quality and/or viability of a product or service, while giving the reasons why the public should choose the product or service against many others.
3. Recall the existence of a product or service already on the market.

It is said the reason for which we prefer hen's eggs over that of a duck's, is that the hen will sing before laying an egg (it's advertising its product) while the duck will lay in absolute discretion (no publicity here).

Advertisement – The decision to advertise a product is divided in two (2) categories; developing the message and selecting the medium.

Advertising Campaign – The planning of an advertising campaign is based on the following considerations:

*   Determine the objective of the campaign (inform, persuade

or recall).

- Establish a budget for advertising which is based on the percentage of sale (i.e. Cosmetics – 18% of revenues).
- Creation of the message – (trials are required prior, during and after the product/service is on the market).
- Selecting a medium by answering the following questions;

1. Who is the consuming public;
2. Which media category (i.e. printed or audiovisual medium);
3. Which media vehicle could reach the consumer more effectively (i.e. radio/television programs, magazine, newspaper-section, etc.)
4. What is the time-frame to better reach the consumer (i.e. what time of day do you want your message to reach the consumer);

- Measure the results – it is important to gage the feedback of the consumers (Pilot sales, detachable coupons, mail-rebates, etc.)

Public Relation – It describes the 'positive image' of the product, company, service or person that you create through forms of communications which are free. The aim of the 'public relation' is to influence the opinion, the perception or the trust placed in an organization by its public (clients, shareholders, government agencies, consumers, etc.).

- **Press material** – Creating material for the written press (press/news releases, press kits, informative documentation, etc.).
- **Special Events** – Create publicity around special events which are sponsored by the organization (seminars, conferences, competitions, anniversaries, etc.). The objective is to create a forum to propagate information regarding the organization addressing directly the public concerned and constituents.
- **Speeches/Presentations** – Organize and make speeches/presentations in front of industrialists, influential groups, and which are addressed to people susceptible to show an

interest in your organization.

- **Public Service activities** – Create opportunities to establish or to support community initiatives which benefit from society and which could engender publicity or other form of communications profitable to your organization. For example; a company which sells computers would sponsor IT education or donate computers to the schools of their choice.
- **Promotional material** – Develop annual reports, brochures, pamphlets, bulletins, audiovisual presentations, etc. geared to maintain a continuum of information distribution to your public, partners, government agencies, and to you donors.

Public relation can support the launching of a product, the promotion of a product or service. But it is also there to defend the cause of your organization and to engender and maintain 'a good impression' in the public eye.

Press Release

The press release is the 'appetizer' sent to the press giving them a 'taste' of what coming… It allows you to express an opinion or to take a stand in regards to the position your organization will adopt vis-à-vis of such or such event. Generally it relates to:

- The organization's reaction when faced with a certain situation;
- The organization taking a stand or rectifying its position;
- The organization's right to respond to any article published in the press.

These press releases are usually accompanied of two types of instructions: "embargo" or "for immediate publication".

Press-release under "embargo" – they determine the date at which the information should be released to the public. Some organizations as well as governmental agencies, or international institutions or companies use this form of press release in order for the press to have time to read the content of a speech (for example), or of an announcement that will be made during an event occurring at a certain date in the future (i.e. the speech that will be pronounced by the president of your organization on the occasion of the Annual Convention opening ceremony on date of....).

Press-release "for immediate publication" – as the title implies, this is a press release containing information destined to be delivered to the public immediately. There are better issued when they discuss or announce the stand your organization is taking vis-à-vis a given situation or event.

Publicity and media

Publicity is an investment into the future of your organization. It is therefore important to know how to determine the type of publicity and which of the media group to choose in order to attain your public effectively at reasonable costs. Each medium has its characteristics which are their assets or their limitations.

Publicity in the newspapers – Newspapers and daily tabloids are sold at the corner store, through annual subscription, or in the 'news-boxes'. People generally read the paper to obtain more details about the information they have already heard on the radio, seen on television or through the word of mouth. In the paper there is a bit of everything for everyone; news, sports, games and leisure, entertainment, arts, culture, classifieds, crosswords, etc. You can attain your targeted public in placing an ad in the section of the paper which is susceptible to attract their interest. People buy the papers often for one reason or another – to read the news, get the sports scores and comments, read the editorials or go through the classifieds, etc.

As opposed to the radio or television, the newspapers give the reader the opportunity to peruse his favorite section (or the entire paper) at leisure – in the bus, train, subway or at home, etc. The newspapers' publicity is more detailed inasmuch that it gives the price of a product or service, the address and phone numbers of a company.

The newspaper offers the advertisers very flexible costs. You can choose an advertisement in function of your budget.

Disadvantages of the newspaper advertising

Newspapers have limitations which you'll do well to keep in mind.

- Newspapers have a very short lifespan – they are only kept for a day or two.
- Generally the newspaper readers are older.
- They're not of the highest print quality, especially when reproducing photographs is concerned. The drawings or graphics are better suited to newspaper publication.
- The page's dimension of a paper is generally large; therefore, the small classifieds or advertisements have a tendency to appear insignificant against the size of the page and to pass unnoticed.
- Your advertisement is always in competition with others.
- There is no guarantee that everyone who buys the paper will read your advertisement – many will not read the section in which your advertisement is place. Others will skip the page of your advertisement because 'there's nothing good to read in there'.
- Contrary to a magazine, the paper is only read by one individual.

Important to remember

Don't forget to include the name, logo, address and telephone number of your organization in your advertisement.

'The place' of your advertisement is very important – indicate clearly in which section your advertisement is to appear.

It's an accepted rule of thumb that your advertisement could appear three to five times before loosing its impact.

Publicity in the magazines

There are two categories of magazines; professional and commercial.

Professional magazines – These are publications which are designed for a professional readership such as businesses, services, industries, trades, etc. This type of magazines deals with subjects of interest to the members of a particular profession.

Commercial magazines – These are magazines which are destined to the public at large. They are available at the corner store and bookstore or by subscription. It is important, as we have mentioned already, to know which type of magazine would be more suited to reach the targeted readership.

Almost the same criteria that apply to the newspaper will apply to the magazines – at the exception of:

- Having a longer life span – magazines are published monthly or weekly and people have a tendency to collect the issues.
- Printing the photographs (in color) and the paper used are of much higher quality.
- The advertisements being centered on the quality of the image rather than the text.
- Magazine advertisement being often in color.
- The reading of a magazine is done by more than one individual.

Publicity on the radio

The radio offers the audience the freedom to hear (or listen to) your advertisement without abandoning what they're doing. Most people will listen to the radio going to and from work.

Advantages

- Radio advertising is a relatively cheap way to attain the public. It is called the "Theater of the Mind" because the voices you hear can create a picture, a scene, or an image which would be extremely costly if reproduced by visual effects.

- You can change the content of a radio advertisement very easily.
- The radio announcers generally have friendly relations with their audience. Using these announcers to promote your organization is almost, in itself, an endorsement of your organization.
- Radio advertisement can also support your newspaper or magazine publicity (e.g. read our ad in such or such magazine or paper on October 2...)

Limitations

- The audience cannot listen to an advertisement twice in a row – some times it will take days before they hear it again. Once 'gone to air' it's done; gone...
- There is a proliferation of radio stations. The audience cannot listen to every one of them at the same time. The advertiser is often forced to pass his ad on several stations in the hope to attain his audience.
- People don't listen to the radio all the time. One must take into account the 'prime-time hours' (i.e. between 6:00am and 10:00am – when people get ready or go to work and between 3:00pm and 7:00pm – when people drive home).
- You cannot broadcast more than one 'notion' at a time (two at the most) in a radio announcement. And it's not the best place to give your phone number – unless you repeat it three or four times; in which instance the listener will remember the phone number but not the message.
- Remember the '*Rule of Three*' when advertising in the radio. Your listener will need to hear *three times* your message (or any part of it) before assimilating and retaining its content. Therefore you will need to repeat the highlight of your message three times to be effective.

Publicity on television

TV is considered as the Queen of Media when it comes to advertising, because people will spend more time in front of a

TV screen than reading the paper or listening to radio. Television combines visual effects to color, sound and animated images; but if it is the most effective of all media, it is also the most costly.

Advantages
- The images are animated.
- It attains the targeted audience easily (i.e. your can reach the men while they watch the news or sports, the children while they watch cartoons and the women while they watch their favorite soap operas).
- There are endless possibilities with a camera – you can take the audience everywhere.
- You can attain the masses – thereby the pseudonym of 'mass-media'.

Limitation
- The cost of publicity on TV is sometimes 10 to 30 times higher than that of the radio.
- The cost varies depending on the targeted audience and the programming length and the hour of diffusion (i.e. prime-time ads will cost more than others.)
- The advertising spot must be of high quality. The viewers have become extremely demanding in regards to the quality of the 'commercials'. A bad quality ad will have a negative effect on the message contained in the ad.
- Your ad is in competition with other ads and their content which are on the air at the same time.
- As in the radio, the message comes and goes. The viewer will not see your message again unless you pay for a second diffusion.
- The people, who watch TV, use the 'commercials' to change channels, to go and get a sandwich, or be distracted from watching the screen.

Publicity through 'direct mailing'
The publicity through 'direct mailing' is by far the best means to consolidate the constituency of an organization. Direct mail, as

its name implies, consists of publicity material being distributed via the regular postal service. But that same material can also be distributed by couriers or volunteers. There are two type of 'direct mail': "personalized mail" and "non-personalized mail".

Personalized mail – It is suggested that you used this form of direct mailing when addressing correspondence to major donors or addressing philanthropic foundations – for example, a letter of solicitation or recognition for the donors or foundations' generosity.

Non-personalized mail – These are form of correspondence addressed to the public at large soliciting funds, invitations, announcements, etc.

General rules
- Adapt the message to the targeted audience.
- Keep your address book up-to-date.
- Enclose a self-addressed envelope (to your organization).

Publicity 'gadgets'
The publicity gadgets comprise all items, such as T-shirts, pens, bags, calendars, agendas, pins, bookmarks, etc., which are distributed to the public during events such fairs, expositions, festivals, conferences, conventions, seminars, etc. These items often display your logo, your 'slogan', perhaps your address, phone numbers or other relevant information.

Business cards – The business card is the first item and I would even go as far as saying 'the most important item' comprised in the publicity 'gadgets'. You must carry enough business cards on you where ever you go (you never know who you shall meet in your travels). You need to take as many as you give and even more than that. They'll give you an idea who's who in your entourage.

General rules
- Choose those items that best represent or symbolize your organization.

- Adapt these items to the taste of the targeted population. For example agendas for the professional person and T-shirts for the students.
- As much as possible, include the name, the logo, the telephone number and the address of your organization.

Message

The message you need for the public you need

When the daughter of one my friends reached her thirteenth birthday she demanded to be 'excised'. Her reasons – her friends were mocking her because she was not excised. The messages, from the NGO's, that are fighting against excision (female genital mutilation), are geared towards the women who perform this type of surgery. They assume these women are the cause behind the continued practice. Like my friend's daughter, if the message had been addressed to the young ladies, the ones who are potential victims, there would have been a better chance for the message to have the desired effect. In the case of excision, as long as the young women are not sensitive or au-fait with the damaging effects of this practice, the battle will be very difficult to win.

Choosing the proper age level to which the message is addressed is the most effective way for a message to have an impact on the public. For example in the case of excision, the message was oriented more towards the women who performed the surgery and less towards the young ladies in school or learning institutions. Even if the women performing the surgery were disposed to abandon the practice as long as they have a child coming to them they will continue trading.

In the case of excision, it would be wise to measure the results in function of numbers and percentages.

- How many women have abandoned the practice;
- How many of these have been re-integrated into other trades (this would be designed to encourage the women who have not yet abandoned the practice to do so and to motivate

donors to support the program).

- How many women have escaped from excision because of the education provided to mothers and daughters alike?

Illustrate the results of your findings with the testimonies from beneficiaries

Inform the public of the impact your program has through the publication of testimonies from beneficiaries in the newspapers, bulletins, brochures, pamphlets, activity reports, ceremonies, speeches, etc. Of course you need to select the testimonies that represent best the beneficiaries as a whole and in particular, those that will give life to the impact your actions have on the public. Testimonies allow to break down taboos, and motivate the ones who 'have not made up their mind yet' on whether or not to participate in your program. A good example is to take the testimony of a reformed drug-addict and introduce it to the most vulnerable section of the population when you have a program that addresses that cause.

The testimonies from beneficiaries – allow the targeted population to turn their attention to your cause, your program, which is the principal motivation for a donor to support (and maintain support) of a program. In fact it is not the number of persons who attended your seminar which is important in the eyes of a donor, it is the number of people who have been affected or have benefited by your programs. Those are the people who are the multiplying factors of your programs. Again, in the case of excision – the donor will look at how many young ladies have escaped mutilation thanks to your program – that's all…

"Do" and let people talk

As we have mentioned above, an organization needs to establish a plan of Public Relation, a publicity campaign and other form of communications to attract the necessary support for its programs. The role that the Press plays into the success of your communication campaigns is decisive. If you *do* your work conscientiously, one of these days the press will not be able to avoid noticing you.

One morning of January 2001, I received a call from Celeste Williams, a journalist with the "Indianapolis Star". She was soliciting an interview regarding the activities benefiting the African immigrants. We need to remind the reader that at the time of the creation of the "United States African Housing Foundation" and later when we established the "International African Community Council", our means of survival were very limited. Our support depended only on the donations of founding members such as Mamadou Sylla, Aboubakary Keita, Miniimah Cisse and others. For more than two years, without a head-office, most of the organization's operations were managed from my living room. Thus, having made an appointment the journalist came to my house on Monday morning. She followed my steps throughout the day and witnessed the services rendered by our organizations. Her article appeared on the 'First Page' of the 'Local News' section of the "Indianapolis Star" on January 22, 2001 under the title of "He is a Guide and a Friend". It goes without saying that from then on, the article was extremely beneficial to our organization's activities. The rest is 'history'. According to Celeste Williams, the reporter, someone had slipped a memo in her mailbox asking her to take a look at our organization. Being of the trade, when someone attracts the attention of a journalist on you, more often than not it is not for your good looks that they do so. Therefore, 'do and let people talk' is a politic, which can bear its fruit in time.

Factor 4
Formation and Code of Ethics
A sector full of opportunities

In the United States, as in almost everywhere else in the world, one will not ask 'what you know how to do, but what you have learned to do'. To practice most professions, you need a degree. But a degree is not sufficient. In the United States, more often than not, you need to pass an exam to obtain a license or a certificate enabling you to practice certain professions. For those professions which demand that you obtain a certificate or a license, the law requires that you post such license or certificate on the wall of the office where you practice that profession. That is to say; in order to put your American partners at ease, it would be recommended for them to know that you have followed the same courses or attended similar institutions of learning as they did and relating to the management of an NGO.

However, the aim of obtaining a formation is not only to put your partners at ease, but it is also to provide a language harmonization and to open the communications channels with them, that much wider. In view of the great number of NGO employees throughout the world, and of the many managers within these organizations, who are desirous to act with professionalism while respecting the Code of Ethics at all times, the formation sessions are also an opportunity for NGO people to acquire further knowledge and to perfect their know-how.

Formation as a source of relation

The formation sessions provide a unique opportunity to renew old relation and make new ones. Your acquired knowledge will allow you to act more effectively, and the relations will open doors to new financing ventures. It is said that a man will give to an NGO for three reasons; (1) because of the relations; (2) for the relations and (3) by the relations. In a few words – it means that relations are the beginning and the end of success for an NGO.

Freshly enrolled as a realty agent at Century 21, the leading company in real-estate in the States, I was asked to attend a formation session held in house and headed by Stuart Sobel; a retired (Internal Revenue Service) man who had spent thirty years in the United States' Tax Department. During one of our conversation, Stuart Sobel informed me that he was the founder of a consulting firm which dealt mostly with NGO's. This news couldn't have come at a better time. To date I can't recall the subject of the session, but I can recall that meeting Stuart Sobel was the best thing that happened during the event. In fact, when I came to the States, I had a dream – I wanted to increase my knowledge in the field of management of NGO's. After knocking at every door in quest of someone who could help us, my friends Mamadou Sylla, Aboubakary Keita and I, found in Stuart Sobel, the man who could make our dream a reality.

Given that the NGO's cover every socio-economic sector of our society, the formation session are venues where you find people with immense resources. Lecturers as well as participants represent foundations, government agencies, religious congregations, etc. Even if you think that you're not going to learn much at one of these sessions, you could meet many people who could be very useful to your organization, as such was the case when I met Stuart Sobel at Century 21 training session.

Why the formation?

We say that a child goes to school for two reasons; (1) the fear of the punishment and/or (2) the hope for a reward – and that the adult attends courses for the only reason that he is due to attend classes. In other words, an adult has a goal, and to attain that goal he needs to acquire knowledge – or only to prove that he attended that particular course. For example, the law in the United State demands that, to renew a professional license, you attend a number of hours in class. This particular formation is known as "Continued Education".

The first time I attended a "Continued Education" formation session in order to renew my real-estate license in the State of Indiana, I was surprised to see that many of the participants had their laptop (computer) open and numerous files spread about their desks. While the instructor was carrying on with his lecture, the gentlemen at the back of the room carried on 'with business as usual!' And the instructor paid no attention to them. I was to learn later that these men had attended the course only to obtain a certificate saying that they, in fact, 'attended classes'. Since the law demanded that they attend classes – they went to the course and sat through the eight hour session. In the end the instructor couldn't do otherwise than giving them the certificate in question which attested that they 'attended classes'.

In fact it is not only in the States where attending courses is required for a person to acquire fresh knowledge in his profession. George T. Benson, of the Ivory Coast Television Broadcasting Corporation knows something about that.

George T. Benson was one of the best Show Host on the Ivory Coast television. He had led many young people to taking their first steps in the world of the audiovisual. Among his pupils was a young Frenchman. Much later, and after the young men had returned to his country, George Benson and several of his colleagues from the Ivory Coast television and radio were sent to France for a formation session. It was a total surprise for George Benson to see that the very same young Frenchman he had taught some years earlier was now standing at the podium and that he was the session instructor. George packed his bags and went home, because according to him, he couldn't learn very much from the instructor. Upon their return to Ivory Coast, his colleagues, who had stayed for the length of the course, received promotions and accolades for their increased performance through what they had learned in France. The only person, who didn't get a raise, a promotion or an accolade, was George Benson.

Never underestimate the opportunity that formation could offer you.

Conditions of the donations

For the charitable organization to donate funds, it has to be assured that you have the necessary expertise to execute the project for which the donation is made. Therefore it is necessary for you to have the professional qualifications to carry out the task responsibly.

For example, if your medical knowledge allows you to become a reputable practitioner in the area of sexually transmissible diseases it does not automatically follow that you would be able to handle the complex management of an NGO. In fact most NGO's with immense potential either fail or stagnate because the people at the helm do not have adequate formation to assume the proper management of an NGO. Managing an NGO is not all advocacy, lobbyism, and activism it is also managing the very diverse form of fund collection, communication, techniques of collection, public relation, marketing, strategic planning, organization of special events, while always recognizing the value of its participants and donors.

The role your formation plays in your success

It is said that of ten people who succeed in their given profession, nine have followed a formation corresponding to that profession. The tenth person is naturally blessed – everything he/she touches will turn to gold. But it is better not to rely on Lady Luck and to count on your formation to reach your goal. It is also said, that men can succeed where ever he is. However to do so, he needs three things: resources, formation and community support. It is therefore necessary for us, to acquire the knowledge that will enable us to manage the financial or material resources, which will be put at our disposal.

Code of Professional Ethics

The practice of any profession is the source of a code of conduct which is better known as the "Code of Ethics" or Deontology. The practice of any trade is accompanied by certain risks – risk to the public and risk to the profession or trade. We know that there are practices which go beyond the control of the law. That's when the Code of Ethics plays a role and protects the consumers from unwarranted risks or more importantly it will shield the profession from disreputable abuse. The fear of being sanctioned by your colleagues is perhaps more effective than the fear of sanctions from the law. Perhaps you could escape the law, but you cannot escape the Code of Ethics so easily. It is one of the reasons why, in the United States, most of the laws related to professional conduct give ample latitude to the professional organizations when it comes to penalizing their members for breaches of the Code of Ethics. The professionalism demonstrated by NGO managers will be then a source of confidence and credibility for any donor.

A source of employment

One person out of fifteen, in the States, is employed in the NGO sector. We need to acquire NGO management knowledge not only to compete on the market but also to acquire the donor's confidence and trust. The professional capacity demonstrated by a foreign NGO manager will be the determining factor as to the amount of subventions granted to his organization by private foundations, government agencies and individuals. The will of the US government and of the American philanthropist to play a major role in socio-economic development projects in countries of the Third World is no longer to be demonstrated. This is the reason why we need to design formation sessions that respond to the profiles and preoccupations of the American donor.

The objective of the formation should be:

- Create and demonstrate professionalism in the management of NGO's
- Inspire trust and confidence
- Facilitate communication between donors and beneficiaries

Career opportunities in an NGO organization

Hospitals and Educational Institutions (public or private), without being NGO's per se, are areas which attract most charitable donations. These institutions have teams in charge of fund collection. In the United States, millions of employments depend on the NGO sector. And this trend is seen also in countries of the Third World. On top of your academic qualifications, a formation in the NGO management could open many doors. People with a background such as accountants, economists, care givers, health professionals, journalists, etc. are always sought by NGO's and international organizations.

Career opportunities in public and private institutions

Apart from the NGO's, a great number of programs, in public and private institutions offer professional management positions which generally entail:

1. Strategic planning;
2. Program management and animation;
3. Identification of public and private sources of funds;
4. Preparing funding submissions;
5. Daily supervision of fund collection activities;
6. Activity reports preparation and presentation;
7. Executing the decisions emanating from the Board of Directors;
8. Program evaluation and follow-up;
9. Recruitment and placement of volunteers;
10. Consolidation of the constituents' participation, etc.

To have access to public or private funding requires an intricate knowledge of the 'playing field'.

The NGO's professional managers are sought for employment on a 'full-time' or 'part-time' basis or as consultants by public or private institutions such as:

Public or Private Educational Institutions, (from kindergarten to university, going through elementary schools, colleges, high-schools, professional or religious schools, etc.) will need NGO managers to assist in their extension, equipment acquisition, or maintenance programs;

Libraries and Museums and historic monuments and/or natural sites, etc;

Public Institutions and administrations, mayors' office, municipal offices, community centers, ministerial departments, etc;

Private Foundations, Cooperatives, Communities – international institutions or government bodies will need NGO managers to oversee the distribution of funds to their NGO's overseas or to their programs on foreign soil.

Private companies need NGO managers for the management of their charitable programs.

Sports organizations (football, basket-ball, boxing, etc.) will use NGO managers for their public relation tasks such as talking to their fans, supporters, and for the management of funding campaign programs.

Many are the public and private institutions and other government organizations in Third World countries, counting among the categories mentioned above, which are ignorant of the financial funding programs that exist and that are based on private funds such as individual, special events, private foundations, cooperatives, communities, etc. – As well as on government organizations such as "United States Agency for International Development" (U.S.A.I.D.) and many others – actually too many to be listed here.

Using the services of professional NGO managers for fund raising administration could open new horizons for a good number of institutions or public organizations.

People with a background, an expertise and an extensive knowledge in the management of NGO's and their fund raising or campaigns have many career opportunities opened to them.

Factor 5
Sources of Financing
Knocking at the right door

The Salvation Army, a public charity organization, recently announced that they had received a donation of $1.5 billion from Mrs. Joan Kroc (deceased on October 12th in San Diego at the age of seventy-five). Mrs. Kroc was the widow of Mr. Ray Kroc, the owner of the "McDonald" food chain. Mr. Kroc was well known for his philanthropic works. Donations could be of only one dollar or be made of huge sums amounting to several millions of dollars, such as the one mentioned above. The donations made to NGO's are issued from five principal sources: Individuals, Foundations, Corporations, Patrimonies (or Legacies) and from other governmental sources.

Contribution Sources
In 2002 the American NGO's have benefited from donations totaling $212 billions. The principal sources of financing were:

- Individuals for 75% or $161 billions;
- Foundations for 12% or $26 billions;
- Corporations for 5% or $9 billions;
- Legacies, Patrimonies and other governmental sources for 8% or $17 billions.

The contributions made by type-organizations

The contributions received can be classified by type-organizations receiving the donations – these are:

1. Religious organizations for 38% or $81 billions
2. Educational institutions for 15% or $32 billions
3. Humanitarian organizations for 10% or $21 billions
4. Health organizations for 8% or $18 billions
5. Arts, Culture and Humanity for 5% or $12 billions
6. Public entities for 5% or ~ $11 billions
7. Environmental concerns for 3% or $6 billions
8. International organizations for 2% or $4 billions
9. Donations to the foundations for 12% or $26 billions.

Contributions from Individuals

The contributions made by individuals are by far the biggest source of donations. It represents 75% of the total purse. The small contributors are in abundant numbers, the big donor is rare. But, the efforts to obtain any sort of donations must be concentrated on the 'big donors'. We must always keep in mind the 20/80 rule.

The 20/80 rule – A philosopher said that for a project to succeed, it is necessary for 20% of the efforts made, to cover 80% of the needs – thereby the 20/80 rule. For example, let's assume that your program needs $10.000, and you are counting on a community of 1000 members to finance your project. The simple way to obtain the $10,000 needed would be to approach each member for a donation of $10. But it is not evident that all of the members will pay their contribution. If that would be the case, you would find yourself with a budget deficit right at the starting line. On the other hand, if you apply the 20/80 rule you would have to identify the 20% of the membership which owns 80% (or better) of the community's resources. In every community, 80% of the resources are in the hands of 20% of the population. Those members are named, in the philanthropic sector, as "Major Donors". Your strategy would be then, to convince the 20% of the community to contribute 80% of the total cost of the project – which would represent $8,000 among 200 members. Thereafter you would have no difficulty to attract individual contribution of $10 per person – If each of the 800 members would contribute their $10, which is not evident, you would receive $8,000 from them or a total donation of $16,000. Even if only half of the 800 people contribute their $10 your goal of $10,000 will be surpassed by far.

Building your "record of achievements"

At the creation of the "Association pour le Développement de la Préfecture de Kerouané (A.D.KER.)" the first concern was to decongestion the classrooms in the elementary school at the center of town. These classrooms were old and usually filled beyond twice their normal capacity. The organization members were very conscious of their limited means, of their lack of experience, and they had no record of accomplishments which could have proved that they had the capacity and capability to organized and execute such a project as the one of constructing a new school. Therefore the executive members decided to restore the school instead.

In the first year, from the member's contributions, the NGO fixed and painted the walls, doors and windows of one classroom. The school counts 12 classrooms.

During the second year, when the NGO approached the economic operators, the children's parents and the general population, and solicited donations for the renovation of their elementary school, the results went beyond anyone's hope. At the end of the campaign the 12 classrooms were restored anew.

During the third year, the NGO approached the governmental organizations in view of financing the construction of a new school in Kerouané. It was without a moment's hesitation that the funds were granted given the NGO's 'record of achievements.'

The first thing to consider, when an organization is desirous to obtain subventions from public charity institutions for its projects or programs, is to build a 'record of achievements' which relates, as much as possible, to the projects or programs for which you seek their support. Many organizations will launch ambitious projects without having any 'records of achievements' in their portfolio. As noble as a project could be, the donors will have doubts when it will come to financing a project presented by novices to the task. The community organizations must take into account, before soliciting any financing for the building of a new infrastructure such as a school, a health center or a library, etc., that the existing building is in good state of repairs. Elaborate a construction project for a new school, when the existing building is in a state of disrepair, will bring the eventual donor to the conclusion that the new school will suffer the same fate as the existing one – as soon as the building will be erected. Donors can make the difference between the lack of maintenance and the lack of funds. That is why the NGO at Kerouané refurbished the existing elementary school thereby demonstrating not only their capability at being a match to the task, the gaining of community support but also building their 'record of achievements' which ultimately provided them with the necessary funding for the construction of a new school.

The Patrimonies or Legacies

Patrimonies and Legacies constitute one of the most important sources of donations in the United States. In fact, a large number of people, at the end of their life will legate their fortune to NGO's to carry out philanthropic works. Some people negotiate the terms of their legacy with the beneficiary organizations – the donations then is often made in terms of annual grants, monthly annuities or any form of 'planned giving'. Others, legate their estate to an organization without informing the latter of their intentions, such was the case for the "National Public Radio (NPR)", when the board of director of this corporation was informed that they had just been named the beneficiaries of a legacy amounting to $200 million from the late Mrs. Joan Kroc – One can just imagine the surprise that announcement created! During her lifetime NPR never benefited from Mrs. Kroc's donations and although she was a faithful listener of KBSP in San Diego, her decision to will that portion of her fortune to NPR was one made at the last moment, because and according to her entourage, Mrs. Kroc had been very appreciative of the NPR reports on the Iraqi war in 2003. Mrs. Kroc's estate is valued at nearly $2 billions, which puts her in 121st place among those listed in the "Fortune 500" in Forbes Magazine. Among others, who were named beneficiaries of Mrs. Kroc's fortune, were the University of San Diego and the Université Notre Dame, which received $50 millions each.

The donor's appearance is not to be trusted

The book entitled "The Millionaire Next Door" describes the profile of the real millionaire. It is not always the one who lives in a mansion, drives a Mercedes or a Rolls Royce, smokes cigars and dresses to the hilt, who is the 'real millionaire'. From investigations carried out by the author of the book, the real millionaire is very often a modest fellow. He lives in an apartment, eats in restaurants or at the counter of a fast food chain, drives a second-hand car, etc. If you're not careful the opportunity would pass you by – as it was the case for the Director of Harvard University – (See 'Introduction').

The different types of Foundations

As opposed to contributions made by individuals, the donations made by the foundations are more consistent as to the amount allocated or as to the sectors benefiting from their contributions. Foundations are much easier to locate and their donations are not often unexpected. Generally they respond to the demand for subventions which are submitted to them.

The term 'foundation' is used to describe a variety of charity organizations. The main function of a foundation is to subsidize the programs or projects of non-governmental organizations, which are seeking their support. There are several types of foundations, among those we will list but a few.

- Private Foundation
- Corporate Foundation

- Community Foundation
- Operational Foundation
- Foundation by name only
- Endowment Foundation
- Funds, etc.

The Private Foundations depend generally on one source of financing (individual, family, or business), and use their revenues from their investments (real-estates, royalties, activities, etc.) to subsidize other charitable organizations. Foundations are the subject of more control and restrictions than other NGO's. It is required that their annual subventions to other NGO's be equal or superior to 5% of their revenues on invested capital. The foundations, such as the Bill Gates Foundation, Ford Foundation, Carnegie Corporation, W.K. Kellogg Foundations are examples of this type of foundations which are subject to such requirements. There are, to date, over 56.000 foundations in the United States.

A Corporate Foundation is a private foundation which receives funds and grants subventions to NGO's in the name of a company. Besides the Corporate Foundation you find some companies which have internal subvention programs; other companies prefer subvention programs in lieu and in place of a corporate foundation.

The Community Foundation is a group of resource donors who focus their subventions on a given region or a city of their choice. They collect charity funds and distribute them to the charity organizations evolving in the chosen areas. They serve as intermediaries between donors and NGO's of a community. They manage funds, assist individuals or other foundations in the appropriate distribution of the subventions or in the choice of the beneficiary NGO. Or they could intervene in the choice of community foundation acting as fund managers for other foundations or as subvention management consultants (e.g. Central Indiana Community Foundation).

- **Fund Management** – The donor entrusts to the foundation, funds said to be 'restricted' or 'unrestricted' and demands that the foundation selects, distributes these funds to the projects or programs chosen. The donor also requires that the foundation follows-up on the proper execution of these programs or projects by the recipients as well as assumes all administrative duties associated with the management of these funds.

- **Donor-Advised** – The foundation assists and counsels the donor in the choice of recipients and in the execution of all administrative formalities associated with the donation. The final decision resides with the donor at all times.

- **Restricted Funds** – William E. English was a visionary philanthropist living in the Indianapolis community in the early 1900's. After his death in 1926 and that of his widow in 1936 his entire estate went to "The Indianapolis Foundation". In his testament, Mr. English made provision for the construction of a building that would house charitable organization offices. "The English Foundation Building" located at 615 North Alabama Street was erected in 1956 thereby fulfilling Mr. English's last wishes. Today, the edifice serves as head-office for the Central Indiana Community Foundation, The Indianapolis Foundation, The English Foundation and a dozen other charity organizations dedicated to community services. Some donors, when it comes to legate their estate add riders or clauses to their will to specify the conditions of distribution of their fortune. These clauses (or restrictions) can be geographic – *"the funds will only be allocated to programs of organizations which evolve and have an impact on such or such city, area or community"*. For example; "Central Indiana Community Foundation". The 'restrictions' can also be demographic – *"the funds will be allocated to those community groups of such or such ethnicity"*. Or the restrictions will apply to a certain sector of activities – *"the funds are destined to programs pertaining to the arts, music, health, scholarship, research, etc"*.

- **Unrestricted Funds** – A number of donors, when they were involved with a certain philanthropic activity before their passing, will not impose restrictions when it comes to their legacy. However, they may have had some preferences for a zone or another, for a sector or another, or for a particular group or another, and that for efficiency reasons or simply because they had a particular interest in a certain area of activities.

Operational Foundation – These foundations use their funds for the financing of their own charitable operations – instead of allocating subventions to other organizations; (for example the Carnegie Endowment for International Peace and the Getty Trust). Some hospitals and public universities, etc. create annexed organizations which will adopt the name of "foundation" to support their operations. These foundations do not grant any subvention to other organizations. In effect they are instruments of fund solicitation which collect donations from various sources in order to support the parent institution. Some charitable organizations will include the term "Foundation" in their name although they will not allocate or distribute funds to anyone.

'Endowments'
The 'Endowments' are governed by the same regulations as those regulating the private foundations.

'Funds'
The 'Funds' have the same status as the private foundations; most often, they entrust their administration into the hands of the community foundations.

Foundation "In Name Only"
The Foundations "In Name Only" are non-governmental organizations which include the term "Foundation" into their name for various reasons – although they have no funds to distribute or to allocate to other organizations as it is the case for the other type of foundations. For example the "United States African Foundation" is the operational name or *assumed business name* of the "**United States African Housing Corporation**". The organization adopted the term 'Foundation' to facilitate its public relation efforts and to emphasize the fact that it is a 'non-profit' organization.

Some suggestions to keep in mind when talking to a foundation

To help the foundation to attain its objective in the long term, we need to determine if the objective is to allocate or distribute funds to:

- Specific activities;
- Attain specific goals;
- Reach specific groups of people/population;
- Certain types of organizations;
- Specific geographic areas;
- Some specific areas of interest;

And it would be recommended to:

- Identify the key personnel and to determine which/who were the recipients of previous grants in examining the foundation's report or tax return for previous years.
- Solicit, in writing, the forms and directives necessary to obtain a grant – address the correspondence to the Program Officer of the foundation.
- Enter in contact with previous (or current) recipients to obtain relevant information concerning the process.
- Enter in contact with the Program Officer of the foundation to obtain information concerning the directives to be followed.
- Each foundation has its own protocol. The most important thing to remember when you wish to obtain a grant from a foundation is to be *patient*. It is therefore recommended to establish a relationship between your organization and the foundation of your choice. The process is slow, but at length it will be profitable to both your organization and the foundation of your choice.
- Never criticize another organization (in competition with you) in front of members of the foundation.

Corporations

The amount of the donations made by corporations is commensurate with their net profit. When business is good, donations increase; when business is bad, donations decline drastically. To benefit from the support given by corporations you need to be able to demonstrate the positive impact which your programs will have on their activities. Corporations are only interested in 'profitable philanthropy'. They want to know how your programs could benefit their enterprises. Therefore, it is necessary to show the effects your programs will have on their business.

- The image portrayed by the corporation in the community;
- The positive reputation the corporation has (or will have) in the community;
- The amelioration of the environment surrounding the corporation's operations (better transport, communications, ecology, etc.)
- Offer new opportunities (access to new resources or to new markets, etc.);
- Increase efficiency (formation, raise interest, organize cultural or sport's activities, etc.).

One must remember that the business world will not support programs of which the outcome is unknown or the bases not well established.

Some suggestions to keep in mind when dealing with a corporation

When dealing with a corporation, you need to start with small projects, especially if you don't have a 'record of achievements' to show them.

Don't ask for money – ask for useful items instead; such as computers, food, T-shirts displaying their logo which will be worn by members of your organization during sport's or cultural activities or by volunteers; etc. It is also necessary to establish a rapport with the key personnel in charge of granting subventions on behalf of the corporation. And, you need to obtain external support from people outside your organization, who will endorse your request for funding your projects by corporations.

Governmental Sources

The Federal Government has several subvention programs destined to subsidize NGO's. The principal sources of information in order to have access to these subventions are:

- Printed information – newspapers, magazines, specialized publications, etc.;
- Internet;
- Data Bases;
- Organization Networks;
- Libraries;
- Philanthropic Foundations, etc.

Religious Ministries

The 'Ministries' are religious organizations engaged in public charity works; e.g. distribution of food, medicine, clothes or equipment and undertaking construction projects.

'Ministries' are different from 'worship's place such as churches, mosques, synagogues, temples, etc.; although the ministries are created by the members of a given congregation to execute humanitarian works either within their community or in other communities of their choice.

Process and steps to be taken to request a grant from a foundation

1. Preliminary 'funding request' letter
2. Responding correspondence to the foundation relating to your initial 'funding request' letter
   a) Favorable answer
   b) Unfavorable answer.
3. Letter confirming grant
4. Half-way report
5. Final report.

Preliminary 'funding request' letter

This letter must follow initial contact with the Program Officer of the foundation – this, for him/her to remember your organization and to pay particular attention to your request when he/she is in receipt of your correspondence. Foundations receive hundreds 'funding request' letters, and yours could pass unnoticed if you have not taken care to establish a rapport with the Foundation's officers.

The preliminary letter must describe *briefly* the object and the mission of your organization.

You must describe in a comprehensive and *concise* manner the program for which your organization requests subvention from the foundation. Don't forget that your program must respond to the objectives of the foundation; the goal to attain, geographic zone where its centers its activities, demographic considerations, etc. In fact, your request must respond to the interests served by the foundation.

If you write a 'funding request' letter to a corporation, the impact of your program on the activities of the said corporation must be evident – don't confuse the issue; corporations have no time to waste. (See sample form)

Response letter from the foundation to your preliminary request for funding

You must expect to receive either one of two replies; favorable or unfavorable.

Favorable response

If the reply to your letter is favorable you will be asked to make a final submission (grant proposal). Please note that each foundation has its particular protocols and procedures, but generally, the organizations which have been selected to make a final submission will be invited to attend an 'information session' where the foundation's representatives will;

- Give you the 'Funding Request Forms'

- Give you the directives to follow as well as the material relevant to the interests of the foundation (or corporation)
- Give you the opportunity to meet with the officers in charge of the program; or those who will assist you in the procedures to be followed
- Give you an idea as to the funding amount which you could expect
- Respond to all of your questions.

It is necessary to work very closely with the Program Officers until the deposit of the funds has been made. They are very cooperative and very attentive. (See sample form)

Unfavorable Response
If the response is unfavorable, don't be discouraged. Enter in contact with the Program Officer in order for you to find out the reasons for the rejection and to receive ampler information pertaining to your demand. The competition is usually extremely close; be competitive and perseverant.

Letter confirming the subvention
After having submitted your final request (grant proposal) in accordance with the directives that you would have received from the Program Officer during the 'informative sessions' you will receive a letter confirming the final decision from the Board of Directors of the foundation (or corporation). The Board of Directors generally ratifies the report which has been submitted to them by the Program Officer.

The confirmation letter will determine:

- The final amount of funding;
- The method and condition of disbursement;
- The objective of the subvention – (what is expected from you);
- The term of the subvention. Please note that any amount of money which has not been expended after the term of the program will have to be returned to the foundation (or

corporation).

- The date at which you will have to submit a report – (Half-Way and Final Report). (See sample form)

Half-Way and Final Reports

These reports have to be submitted in due time. These reports must account for the following:

- Progress made in relation to the objectives set by the program;
- Insufficiencies in relation to the estimates;
- Unexpected difficulties encountered;
- Rate of member's participation;
- Value of contributions made by members of your organization;
- Lessons learned, etc.

"Funding Request" Preliminary Letter

ACTION AND ACTION COALITION
666 Zeroplus Avenue // Sansouciville, USA

February 12, 20...

Mr. C. M
Espoir Foundation
444 Nullpart Street
Sansouciville USA

Dear Sirs;

On behalf of the Board of Directors, I have the honor to request your financial participation into programs and services which will benefit the African Immigrants who are desirous to become active and productive members of our community.

The need for funding from our organization is the result of investigations which have revealed that Africans have much difficulty in settling in the United States; and this because of the multitude of information which is necessary for them to acquire, to understand and to assimilate in order to adapt themselves better in their new country. The new comers need assistance from our communities where there are established groups which share their culture, experience and language.

Indianapolis is a wonderful city comprising many community hospitality groups. We hope that you will join the efforts of "Action and Action Coalition" in helping us to assist the increasing number of African Immigrants who disembark on our shores at the rhythm of 50 to 60 people per month in Indiana alone. It is estimated that 10,000 Africans already live here.

Page 2

Apart from of having to learn another language – French being the mother tongue of most African countries, the Immigrants must also familiarize themselves with the multitude of concepts and our 'way of life' which *is* our daily routines. Even a visit to the local physician or to other services, necessitate the assistance of an interpreter.

"Action and Action Coalition" is an organization established under Section 501(c)3 of the Federal Code of Taxation, and which has for objective the distribution of the huge amount of information necessary to the proper settling process of African Immigrants in our country. Our organization brings support, counsel, and organizes educational programs which aim at the integration of African people into our communities.

In view of the fact that "Action and Action Coalition" is in the primary phase of its endeavors, the funds required will assist the organization in meeting its needs in office space and equipment, payment of salaries, acquisition of educational material (aimed at the education of the Immigrants) and in providing adequate professional services. We require a funding in the amount of $45,000. A formal submission will be made at your request.

Your generous donation and the support you may bring to our program designed to assist in the settling of African people in our country will be much appreciated.

Should you require additional information, please don't hesitate to contact me at my residence – (317) 800-0000.

Sincerely,
Your Name
President, and on behalf of the Board of Directors.

Favorable Response
Letter from the Foundation in response to your preliminary request for funding
(Invitation to make a final 'Funding Submission')

Better Espérance Foundation
444 Nullpart Street // Sansouciville USA

February 12, 20…

Mr. M. C.
Action and Action Coalition
666 Zeroplus Avenue
Sansouciville, USA

Dear Mr. Cisse

We will expect to be in receipt of your submission in time for our meeting of the Board of Director which will be held on November 7, 20… All submissions must be received at our head office at **444 Nullpart Street** (unsealed post) by Friday September 7th, 20… at the latest.

All of the organizations desirous to prepare a submission are invited to participate in our information session scheduled for Thursday July 12, 20… at 8:30am (until 11:00am) to be held at our head office (address mentioned above) in our conference rooms number 6 and 7.

During this information session, the Foundation personnel will distribute the material necessary for you to make a submission. They will also offer suggestions as to the manner in which we would like you to complete the submission, they will also respond to all of the questions relating to the process and follow-up of the submission.

Page 2

We encourage the attendance of the people not only responsible for making the submission but also those persons who will be responsible for the execution and follow-up of your program. (See attachment for information regarding reservation.)

We expect that you will attend this meeting. Should you have any queries regarding the above or the information session, please feel free to contact the undersigned at (317)-000-0000

Sincerely,
The Program Officer

Unfavorable Response
Letter from the Foundation in response to your preliminary request for funding

Better Espérance Foundation
444 Nullpart Street // Sansouciville USA

February 12, 20…

Mr. M. C.
Action and Action Coalition
666 Zeroplus Avenue
Sansouciville, USA

Dear Mr. Cisse

We are writing in response to your preliminary request for funding of your program. However, we regret to have to inform you that your submission was not selected among the organizations that will be awarded funding at this time.

The Foundation has received 218 submissions for a total of $31 millions for this funding cycle. The competition was very close; we have invited 46 organizations to submit their funding requests – for a total of over $5.9 millions.

You can expect to be informed this autumn as to the recipients that would have been selected for funding during the current cycle.

We wish you every success in your endeavor and compliment you in your valued efforts. We thank you for the interest you have shown in our Foundation.

Sincerely,
The Director of Subvention Programs.

**Letter from the Foundation to the recipient organization
Confirmation of Subvention – Example 1**

**Better Espérance Foundation
444 Nullpart Street // Sansouciville USA**

February 12, 20…

Mr. M. C.
Action and Action Coalition
666 Zeroplus Avenue
Sansouciville, USA

Dear Sir;

By this letter, I wish to confirm our recent telephone conversation regarding the fact that our Board of Directors, during their meeting on date of September 13, 20… has approved a subvention in the amount of $45,000 to the **Action and Action Coalition**. These funds will be dedicated to the support of your personnel and to assume the cost of the operations associated with your program.

The subvention will take effect at the reception of the signed agreement and will expire on October 31, 20… The subvention will be paid on or before October 22, 20… - if your signed agreement has been received in our offices by that date. Your reports regarding the distribution of the funds and full accounting are expected on, or before June 1st, 20… and on, or before November 30, 20…

Page 2

When you submit your reports, we ask that you report on the following results:

- The number of new African Immigrants who have obtained an identity card and a driver's license;
- Increase in number of Immigrants who have been employed regularly for 90 (or more) consecutive days;
- The number of Immigrants who have obtained permanent lodgings;
- The development of your organization.

During the meeting of the recipients on date of October 2, 20... the Foundation personnel will provide you with two copies of our agreement and a manual to assist you in the execution of your program which is the subject of our subvention.

You will need to read attentively all documentation provided during the meeting and to return one copy of our agreement – signed; to Mary as soon as possible.

Sincerely,

The President
Program Officer.

Letter from the Foundation to the recipient organization
Confirmation of Subvention – Example 2

Better Espérance Foundation
444 Nullpart Street // Sansouciville USA

February 12, 20…

Mr. M. C.
Action and Action Coalition
666 Zeroplus Avenue
Sansouciville, USA

Dear Sir,

By this letter I wish to confirm our recent telephone conversation relating to the fact the **Action and Action Coalition** has been granted a subvention in the amount of $40,000. This subvention is to be used to pay the salary of one person employed on a part-time basis ($15,000); to purchase office equipment such as computer and accessories ($10,000), and to pay the salary in equal amount (1:1) of a second person employed on a part-time basis – this last portion of the funding will be available during the next calendar year. The **Good Hope Foundation** is happy to support your program thanks to the subvention from the **Hope Fund**.

All reference made regarding the funding granted to your organization will have to be made to the **Hope Fund** under the cover of the **Good Hope Foundation.**

In accepting this subvention, you are agreeing that no individual will benefit personally from the funds granted to your organization and that these funds will not be utilized in any shape, form or manner towards compensating personal, family, or corporation obligations.

Page 2

Your subvention will be effective as at the date of reception of the signed agreement and will expire on October 31, 20... The subvention will be remitted into your bank account on or before October 22, 20... provided that we are in receipt of the signed agreement prior to that date and provided that your documentation relating to the 'Grand Match' Program will have been submitted by that date. Your reports are due on June 1, 20... and on November 30, 20...

During the meeting of the recipients on date of October 2, 20... the Foundation personnel will provide you with two copies of our agreement and a manual to assist you in the execution of your program which is the subject of our subvention.

You will need to read attentively all documentation provided during the meeting and to return one copy of our agreement – signed; to Mary as soon as possible.

Congratulation on your organization being selected for this grant and we hope to continue working with you in the coming years.

Sincerely,

The President
Program Officer

Factor 6
Presentation of a financially viable project
How to write a subvention request

In quest of a subvention

The greatest challenge for a NGO is to convince donors to pay for services rendered to people, who, more often than not, do not know they need the services which will be provided. Between donors and beneficiaries, the ones that receive a service are the ones most difficult to convince.

Therefore, an organization, must not have any other strategy, other priority, and must not take anything for granted if not that of soliciting funding, because it is the sole activity on which depends the success of its programs.

Different types of Projects/Programs

Any study related to the writing of subvention request must begin by acquiring some knowledge as to the different types of projects or programs which are likely to be subsidized.

We must always keep in mind that the institutions do not subsidize an organization just for the nobility of the cause it represents. The institutions subsidize projects or programs which respond closely to the very reason for their existence. The terms 'project' or 'program' are used in a transposable manner. In fact there is only one difference between a project and a program.

What is a Program?

A *Program* is an activity which provides a variety of services which leave *intangible* results in their wake – such as 'Education Program', or 'Social Awareness Program' or 'Health Assistance Program', etc.

What is a Project?

A *Project* is defined as an activity that will leave *tangible* results in its wake. In other words a project may consist in the building or improvement of facilities – such as schools, hospital, recreation centers, etc.

Categories of subvention submissions

Whether they are projects or programs, the institutions will classify the submissions into five (5) categories for which they are ready to give their support.

A. Submission destined to 'engender' a *Program*

The subvention will be assisting your organization to provide services to the community (e.g. an institution (or company) could organize formation programs for adult encompassing some of your organization activities – this is called a *Program Submission*.

B. Submission destined to engender a *Research Program*

1. This type of subventions allows the recipient to conduct a variety of studies dealing with particular subjects – such as 'Cause of the Rural Exodus' or 'Level of Community Support in Urban Areas', etc.

2. This type of subventions also addresses program elaborated for the analyses of results brought about by one treatment or another to a known disease or virus.

C. Submission destined to the receipt of *Technical Assistance*

When an organization recognizes deficiencies in its performance, it can call for a subvention which would entail the engagement of consultants who would assist in redressing the situation and rectify the results towards a more profitable outcome.

The *Technical Assistance* may take the form of *staff formation* or the purchase of new computers, or even entailing a *company re-organization*.

D. Submission destined to the *Planning* or the *Coordination* of certain programs

These submissions cover the cost of the *planning* and of the *coordination* of projects to be elaborated and executed by more than one organization.

E. Submission to increase the *Capital Improvement* of an organization

Commonly called the *Brick and Mortar* submission, this type of subvention will cover the cost of *tangible* projects. That is to say the project will leave tangible traces in its wake such as building renovation or extension, roof replacement, or providing equipment and furnishings for an organization in need.

The steps leading to the writing of a subvention submission (Grant Proposal)

Determine the submission category for which the funds will be requested.

Identify the type of submission among the different types listed above.

Knock at the proper door. Ensure that the institution to which you're addressing your request is in fact financing the type of activities you are intending to fund.

Point to the interest the donor may have in your project. For demands which are addressed to a foundation and which are geared towards a particular sector of the population – the number of people who will benefit from the project/program will be relevant to be introduced in the requests for funding.

Contact the prospective donor. Discuss *frankly* and *openly* your intentions with the Program Officer or with the personnel in charge of funding allocations. Don't confuse the person – be as direct as possible. Request information on the process to be followed – Although, and generally, the foundations or donors ask for the same type of information, the process may vary greatly from one foundation (or donor) to another. If a foundation recommends the use of a particular form (however odd it may appear in your eyes) – use that form and none other.

Obtain the required forms, and get information relating the directives to follow to write the letter of intent and most importantly, make sure you make a note of the date at which 'submissions are closed'.

Write a funding request. (We will give more ample directives regarding this subject later in the book).

Have your request read by a third party before submitting it to the donor or foundation.

Submit your *Request for Funding.*

Evaluation

Programs are usually operations, the results of which are intangible – a least at first glance. They are difficult to measure. In your funding request dossier, which will be addressed to the foundation (or institution), there will be a need to define the evaluation methods to be used in determining the value of the expected results. In the same dossiers and in the reports addressed to the donors it is recommended to avoid using such phrases as: 'to put an end to such or such practice'. No donor is interested in putting an end to a given practice or phenomenon or even to a given situation. What he is interested in however, is to 'reduce or increase' the percentage of something in a given situation. An example of this kind of 'intangible' evaluation can be found in the case of the 'reduction' of the genital mutilation amongst young women – commonly called 'excision'. Some years ago some African NGO's which had made tremendous advances in 'reducing' the devastating effect excising had on the young women's population, announced the voluntary surrender of 'excising knives' by the women who generally performed this kind of operations. I don't think there is a need here to point out that the same 'excising women' would have been acquiring a new excising knife at the first opportunity – after surrendering their first instrument. Therefore this kind of message is useless when it comes to demand further funding in support of this cause – which would have been considered as inexistent since the announcement. The wrongful affirmation of the eradication of a situation is very damaging and prejudices any other organization from demanding further funding for such a *non-existent* cause.

Writing a Subvention Request

The writing of a funding request comprises the following elements;
- 'Summary' (or 'Introduction) describing the object for which the funds are requested;
- Information relating to your organization';
- Formulation of your needs;

1st Step – 'Summary' or 'Introduction'
The introduction must contain the following elements;

- The sum requested;
- Description of the program or project;
- The aim of the program or project.

Bad Example: *The organization "Youth and Development" solicit funding in order to prevent children from loitering in the streets.*

Good Example: *The organization "Youth and Development" solicit the sum of $3,000 to construct a playground in the park at the corner of Independence Avenue and Republic Street.*

Good Example: *The organization "Youth and Development" solicit the sum of $10,000 to organize a vacation program for adolescents. This program will offer educational activities and leisure for 60 young boys and girls between the ages of 7 and 12 who currently live in such (or such area).*

2ⁿᵈ Step – Information related to your organization

The information related to the organization comprises the following data:

- Precise historical details, mission, program/project summary;
- The reasons for which the organization would like to put the program/project in place;
- The size of the neighborhood, locality or community group which will benefit from the program or project (i.e. number of inhabitants).

Bad Example: *The organization "Youth and Development" exist for a number of years and deserve the north part of the city. There are a number of families with children in that area. Our Board of Directors counts 20 members who live in this area.*

Good Example: *The organization "Youth and Development" was created in 1985 and represents 4500 families. Our organization covers an area delimited to the South by Hero Street, to the North by Patriot Avenue, to the West by the Independence Boulevard and to the East by Indian Beach. We have already established a 'neighborhood watch' program; organized a well attended Annual Fete (for the past three years) and we have also planted flower bushes and trees in three of the vacant lots in the area. Approximately 50 people who reside in the neighborhood give of their time (as volunteers) every year to assist in the various activities organized by 'Youth and Development'.*

3rd Step – Formulating your needs

The formulation of the needs for the program or project to be implemented must highlight the following elements:

- Why is the program or project necessary?
- What is subject to problems?
- The statistics in support of your preoccupations.
- The community or local resources available.

Bad Example: *The children living in the neighborhood have a tendency to create troubles because they have nothing else to do.*

Remark: It is not because the children have nothing to do that it is necessary to create a program to occupy their time. There is no need to do something for the sake of doing it. There is however a need to fill the children leisure time with educative activities. Therefore the program must allow the children to draw an educational profit from their leisure time.

Bad Example: *The children of our neighborhood need a playground because there is no other playground of this kind in the area.*

Remark: The lack of a solution to a problem doesn't mean that the solution you are offering is the ideal solution to the problem. You are not building a playground because there are no playgrounds in the area – you are building a playground to allow the children to grow in a favorable environment.

Good Example: *Although there are three parks in the area/ neighborhood, only one of these parks has a playground; the equipment of which is antiquated and dangerous. We have 450 children between the age of 6 and 10 living in our neighborhood...*

Good Example: *The children living in our area are being subjected to some negative influences which are damaging their development and education – i.e. crime level (150 felonies according to the police report of 20...); unwed mother pregnancies on the rise*

(10 babies born from mothers under the age of 16 – according the maternity reports of 20...). During the holidays, most of the children stay home alone because their parents are both at work. Although there are a few vacation programs in place at the moment, there is a long waiting list for the majority of children to have access to these programs. We will offer the children a 'safe' program in a supervised area where they could take computer lessons, improve their reading and writing skills, learn arithmetic, and improve their physical development while participating in sports activities.

Remark: Provide the official source of your statistics.

4ᵗʰ Step – Description of the program or project

The description of the program or project must comprise the following elements:

- The aim of the program or project – what are you trying to accomplish?
- The number of people (provide demographic details) who will benefit from the program or project – be as specific as possible.
- The type of activities encompassed by the program – these activities must be linked to the goal to be attained.
- The impact of your efforts and the indication of positive (negative) results – the ideal is for the efforts and the indications to be measurable (i.e. 80% of the children will know how to use a computer at the term of the program).
- The benefits the program or project will bring to the participants and the impact the program/project will have on the neighborhood, area or locality.
- The method of recruitment of volunteers and program/project participants.
- Why is this program/project the best solution to resolve the problem in question?
- Describe the role of each member of staff and volunteers within the realization of the program/project – who's doing what, where, when?

- The term of the project/program – how long will it take to reach the goal or for the project/program to be realized?
- Community involvement/development.

Bad Example: *We are going to provide the children with fun activities and interesting things to do during the holidays including collage, games, using a computer, sports, arts and crafts. The children will be able to play away from crimes and juvenile delinquency influences.*

Good Example: *The goal of the program/project is to give the families living in the neighborhood a place where their children can play in all tranquility and to allow the children to initiate valuable friendships with other young people living in the area. The playground will comprise swings, a skating rink, mazes, shade trees, trampolines, and a small shelter for the parents. The playground will be laid out in such a fashion that all equipment will be visible from the shelter. We expect that the playground construction will take about two weekends during the month of July 20…and will call on the participation of some sixty (60) volunteers from the neighborhood and thirty volunteers (30) from the local Baptist Church. On the other hand, we expect that this program will encourage the volunteers to continue participating in the programs of the "Youth and Development" organization.*

The impact of this project, in the short term, will see the installation of playground equipment in two weekends time; thereby offering thirty families the use the playground almost immediately after its installation and we expect that at least 60% of the volunteers will continue to participate in our programs.

Good Example: *Our objective is to involve the adolescents living in our area into worthwhile and peaceful activities during the summer holidays. This objective will be reached in giving the children aged between 7 and 12 a place where about sixty of them can find organized leisure and educational activities conducted under qualified supervision. These activities will be held each weekday during the summer holidays.*

Our Program 'Youth Holidays'will be held at the Baptist Church which has given us access to their locals free of charge.

The program will remain in place between July 1ˢᵗ and September 30ᵗʰ and will be open from Monday to Friday from 8:30am to 5:30pm.

Researches have demonstrated that the adolescents need to have locals where they find someone ready to guide them, or where they can receive additional education which complement their school studies or where they have opportunities to interact with adult tutors and with other children of the same age group.

The program will give the opportunity to these adolescents to participate in the following activities:

- *Two (2) tree-planting projects which are due to take place in their neighborhood.*
- *Initiation in the use of a DFP-Micro computer – program organized by the local IT company.*
- *Tutoring mathematics, lectures, word games...*
- *Daily sports activities such as football, volley-ball, swimming, and basket-ball.*
- *Visit of local museum or tourist center in the city – guided tours organized by the community library.*

The two (2) members of staff who will be attending the program on a full-time basis have each more than ten (10) years experience working with children – they will be involved in the coordination of the program. Five (5) neighborhood residents, who have volunteered to participate into the program, will do so in attending the programs on day a week each.

5ᵗʰ Step - The Impact of the Program

Good Example: *We are projecting an amelioration of 50% in reading ability and mathematic comprehension to be seen in the children attending our program. The results will be measurable through the tests the children will take, before and after the program* *and through reports from the responsible instructors. We also expect to see an amelioration of 75% in the youth's athletic performance. This will be measured in their learning of sports rules and ethics based on specific discipline imposed by the instructors. Finally we anticipate, to seeing 75% of the children involved, to participating in two valuable community activities and 75% of them should be able to use a computer at the term of the program.*

The adolescents participating into the program will be recruited from schools and youth associations existing in the area. Our entire neighborhood will benefit from the program inasmuch as the children will be regrouped in a safe place where they will find leisure and educational activities under professional guidance whilst not being left to their own device the summer-through and loitering the streets. Ultimately, we hope that these children will serve as example for other communities to implement similar programs.

We will start recruiting the children and begin the instructors' and volunteers formation on May 1ˢᵗ. The program is due to start on July 1ˢᵗ to continue until September 30ᵗʰ of this year.

6ᵗʰ Step – Collaboration/Partnership

The collaboration with other entities such as organizations, corporations, other community organizations, etc. is viewed favorably by donors. The involvement of other organizations into your program or project adds credibility to it. It will be necessary therefore, to describe the role each organization will play into the program/project. (You will not convince many people that your organization can do everything alone!) Some organizations' leaders dominate their members to such an extent that criticizing them becomes very difficult – it is therefore necessary to have other people from other organizations involved, who will be able to bring constructive criticisms to the subvention submission, the planning and the execution of the project/program.

Bad Example: *Our organization will collaborate with several other organizations in the area and will be involved in the program/ project. We have very good relationships with the presidents of* *each of these organizations and they appreciate what we are doing. Several Churches/Mosques, banks, and a number of small of medium size enterprises are located in our neighborhood.*

Remark: You will have difficulties in convincing a donor of your collaboration/partnership with other organizations if you are not prepared to name them or to describe their involvement into your program or project. You will limit the damages brought by gossips and critics of your program/project from other organizations, which are potential competitors, if you involve them in your program/ project and do not leave them aside at liberty to talk about you behind your back.

Good Example: *The organization "Youth and Development" will execute this program with the collaboration (or in partnership with) the following organizations:*

- *DPS Micro – to ensure InformationTechnology (IT) formation of the children;*
- *Afric-Art will donate 60 T-shirts with the Program Logo printed in front of the garment;*
- *The Baptist Church will provide the locals rent-free;*
- *'Hope Group' who will collaborate with us in the organization of the program;*
- *The South Bakery is prepared to provide food catering for the program once a week.*

7ᵗʰ Step – Evaluation and Evaluation Methods

The follow-up work and evaluation of program/projects are very useful to, and very much appreciated by the donors. The donors want to be ensured that the funds have been used properly and have shown the desired results. If necessary, you would need to attach the evaluation forms to your report files. An evaluation allows the organization to improve on the establishment and conduct of future programs or projects. It also allows the donor to decide knowledgeably on the financing of similar projects that are submitted to them.

Bad Example: *We will ask the children and their parents to tell us if they liked the program and the activities offered during the holidays.*

Good Example: *the Youth and Development Organization (YDO) will evaluate the safety of the playground equipment by asking competent adults to verify the safety of all equipment that will be used by the children. At the end of each day, we will ask the volunteers to fill some reports/forms designed to evaluate if these persons are likely to participate in other projects organized by the YDO. In the weeks following the end of the program/project we will have volunteers going to the park to count the number of families using the playground facilities.*

Good Example: *The evaluation methods used by YDO comprise: pre- and post-tests given by the personnel for each activity encompassed by the program; staff observation and notes; review of projects undertaken or realized by the children participating into the program. At the end of the holidays, we will ask the participants and their parents to fill separate evaluation forms concerning the program and the impact it may have had on their daily routines during the summer holidays. We will use this data to plan the program for the next summer season.*

8th Step – The amount solicited

Reiterate the funding request, giving the exact amount required for the establishment of your project/program

Bad Example: *the YDO counts on your legendary generosity and hopes that you will participate financially into the project/program according to the level of means.*

Good Example: *the YDO solicits your financial participation in this project for an amount of $10,000.*

9th Step – What would you do if you don't receive the requested amount?

It is a very delicate question. Be honest when you give your answer. Decrease the number of participants; or reduce the program's duration, etc.

But, be sure to have 'a fall-back program' in your pocket. If your initial plan does not work you always need to have an emergency exit… The more you demonstrate your obstinacy in attaining your objective the more people will respect you for it and will be prepared to support your endeavors. No one will go to war for a general who has no guts… Certain Foundations require that this problem be addressed within the submission – please note that it is always better to provide more information than necessary (without flooding the plans) and be ready for any and all eventual questions.

Bad Example: *in the case that we should obtain an unfavorable response to our submission we will endeavor to find financing sources elsewhere.*

Good Example: *the YDO has already a portion of the funds and some of the material required for the establishment of the program. Should we not receive a favorable response from you, we will be forced to decrease the program's duration from two (2) months down to one (1) month.*

10th Step – the Budget of the program/project
The budget must be presented in a table format listing the revenues and expenditures expected from the program.

- Ensure that the budget is related to the activities and the information provided regarding the collaboration or partnerships established with other organizations.
- Demonstrate how the amounts were calculated (i.e. 60 T-shirts x $5.00 = $300)
- Give the sources of other revenues and make it clear whether the funds have been received or have been promised.

- Be realistic – give the real costs of the services provided during the programs. Donors will quickly detect if your expenses have been inflated or are inferior to their value. In either case the impression you will impart will not be favorable.
- Make sure that your calculations are correct. (The total of expenses must be equal to the total of revenues.

Bad Example :

Expenditure	In Dollar US ($)
Personnel	10,000
Provisions	3,000
Locals	6,000
Miscellaneous	3,000
Total	**$22,000**

Revenues	
Foundation GT	10,000
Society MTX	3,000
Other Foundations	2,000
Total	**$15,000**

Good Example :

Expenditure	In Dollar US ($)
Personnel	
2 employees x $450/week x 12 weeks	12,000
Taxes	
And benefits (20%)	2,000
Provisions	
$3.00/child x 60 children x 12 weeks	2,160
T-shirts	
60 x $5.00/T-shirt	300

Transport 3 trips x $200/trip	600
Locals	3,000
Telephone $30.00/month x 3 months	90
Food and Catering $3.00/child x 60 children x 60 days	10,800
Insurance 'All-Risks'	1,000
Printing/Photocopying $20/week x 12 weeks	240
Total	**$32,590**

Revenues	En dollars US ($)
In kind	
Foundation GTR (proposal)	3,000
Foundation FFS (submission to be made)	8,000
Society BBT (received)	5,000
Foundation ZZC	7,000
Funds collected by YDO	3,130
In nature	
Baptist Church (locals)	3,000
Society TTR (provision)	1,000
Afric-Art (T-shirt)	300
Foods-Plus ($3/child X 60 children X 12 days)	2,160
Total	**$32,590**

5 volunteers will work, each one day a week, free of charge.

Documents to be enclosed with the submission
- Tax exemption letter re: 501(c)3 non-profit organization

- Board of Directors list of names
- Annual Report or Financial Statements of previous years
- Supporting correspondence from the organizations involved either directly or indirectly into the program or project.

Some suggestions regarding the writing of your subvention submission

The following elements must be clearly legible and heading your documents:

- The name, address, telephone number(s), fax, email(s) and website of the organization;
- Name of the program or project
- Name of the Donor and amount solicited
- Term of funding
- Name, address, telephone number, email, etc of the person who's in charge of the program/project in your organization.
- Include the name of your organization at the bottom of each page of the file;
- Be prepared to answer questions such as:
- "In the long term, what is your plan to finance this project/ program?"
- Don't provide too much information – such as brochures, dozens of letters of support, etc. (As we mention previously 'don't flood your dossier'.)
- Don't use jargon when you write your submission. And don't use any abbreviations. When you use an acronym – give the full name of the organization to which the acronym belongs.

11th Step – Some advice…
- Follow the directives given by the donors. Although the information required are similar, more often than not, the order in which they are to be introduced vary from foundation (or corporation) to foundation.
- Write clearly and succinctly.

- The review process takes time. You must plan everything well in advance.
- Support the revenues 'in nature' (e.g. letter from the Baptist Church re: accessibility to their locals rent-free).
- Always ensure that your accounting is correct.
- Ask someone else to review/read the submission for you.

Example of a Presentation for Program Submission

Youth and Development Organization (YDO)
450 Dormant Avenue
Anystone, FO 46000
Phone: (317) 243-5555 Fax: (317) 243-0000
Project: **"Youth Holiday"**
Submitted to the Marshall Foundation for a sum of $10,000
15 February 200...
Contact: Jean Madal, President SCA, Phone (317) 123-4567

1 – Summary/Introduction
The organization "Youth and Development" solicit the sum of $10,000 to organize a vacation program for adolescents. This program will offer educational activities and leisure for 60 young boys and girls between the ages of 7 and 12 who currently live in such (or such area).

2 – South Community Action
The organization "Youth and Development" was created in 1985 and represents 4500 families. Our organization covers an area delimited to the South by Hero Street, to the North by Patriot Avenue, to the West by the Independence Boulevard and to the East by Indian Beach. We have already established a 'neighborhood watch' program; organize a well attended Annual Fete (for the past three years) and we have also planted flower bushes and trees in three of the vacant lots in the area. Approximately 50 people who reside in the area give of their time (as volunteers) every year to assist in the various activities organized by "Youth and Development".

3 – Formulation of the needs
The children living in our area are being subjected to some negative influences which are damaging their development and education – i.e. crime level (150 felonies according to the police

report of 20...); unwed mother pregnancies on the rise (10 babies born from mothers under the age of 16 – according the maternity reports of 20...). During the holidays, most of the children stay home alone because their parents are both at work. Although there are a few vacation programs in place at the moment, there is a long waiting list for the majority of children to have access to these programs. We will offer the children a 'safe' program in a supervised area where they could take computer lessons, improve their reading and writing skills, learn arithmetic, and improve their physical development while participating in sports activities.

4 – Description of the program/project

Our objective is to involve the adolescents living in our area into worthwhile and peaceful activities during the summer holidays. This objective will be reached in giving the children aged between 7 and 12 a place where about sixty of them can find organized leisure and educational activities conducted under qualified supervision. These activities will be held each weekday during the summer holidays.

Our Program 'Youth Holidays' will be held at the Baptist Church which has given us access to their locals free of charge.

The program will remain in place between July 1ˢᵗ and September 30ᵗʰ and will be open from Monday to Friday from 8:30am to 5:30pm.

Researches have demonstrated that the adolescents need to have locals where they find someone ready to guide them, or where they can receive additional education which complement their school studies or where they have opportunities to interact with adult tutors and with other children of the same age group.

The program will give the opportunity to these adolescents to participate in the following activities:

- *Two (2) replanting projects which are due to take place in their neighborhood.*
- *Initiation in the use of a DFP-Micro computer – program organized by the local IT company.*
- *Tutoring mathematics, lectures, word games...*
- *Daily sports activities such as football, volley-ball, swimming,*

      and basket-ball.

- *Visit of local museum or tourist center in the city – guided tours organized by the community library.*

The two (2) members of staff who will be attending the program on a full-time basis have each more than ten (10) years experience working with children – they will be involved in the coordination of the program. Five (5) neighborhood residents who have volunteered to participate into the program will do so in attending the programs one day a week each – free of charge.

5 – The impact of the program

We are projecting an amelioration of 50% in reading ability and mathematic comprehension to be seen in the children attending our program. The results will be measurable through the tests the children will take, before and after the program, and through reports from the responsible instructors. We also expect to see an amelioration of 75% in the youth's athletic performance. This will be measured in their learning of sports rules and ethics based on specific discipline imposed by the instructors. Finally we anticipate to seeing 75% of the children involved, to participating in two valuable community activities and 75% of them should be able to use a computer at the term of the program.

The adolescents participating into the program will be recruited from schools and youth associations existing in the area. Our entire neighborhood will benefit from the program inasmuch that the children will be regrouped in a safe place where they will find leisure and educational activities under professional guidance whilst not being left to their own device the summer-through and loitering the streets. Ultimately, we hope that these children will serve as example for other communities to implement similar programs.

We will start recruiting the children and begin the instructors' and volunteers formation on May 1st. The program is due to start on July 1st to continue until September 30th of this year.

6 – Collaboration/Partnerships

The organization *"Youth and Development"* will execute this program with the collaboration of (or in partnership with) the following organizations:

- *DPS Micro* – to ensure IT formation of the children;
- *Afric-Art will donate 60 T-shirts with the Program Logo printed in front of the garment;*
- *The Baptist Church will provide the locals rent-free;*
- *'Hope Group' who will collaborate with us in the organization of the program;*
- *The South Bakery is prepared to provide food catering for the program once a week.*

7 – Evaluation – Evaluation Methods

The evaluation methods used by YDO comprise: pre- and post-tests given by the personnel for each activity encompassed by the program; staff observation and notes; review of projects undertaken or realized by the children participating into the program. At the end of the holidays, we will ask the participants and their parents to fill separate evaluation forms concerning the program and the impact it may have had on their daily routines during the summer holidays. We will use this data to plan the program for the next summer season.

8 – The solicited amount

The YDO solicits your financial participation in this project for an amount of $10,000.

9 – What would you do if you don't receive the requested amount?

Please Note: the YDO has already a portion of the funds and some of the materiel required for the establishment of the program. Should we not receive a favorable response from you, we will be forced to decrease the program's duration from two (2) months down to one (1) month.

10 – Budget for the program/project

Expenditure	In Dollar US ($)
Personnel	
2 employees x $450/week x 12 weeks	12,000
Taxes	
And benefits (20%)	2,000
Provisions	
$3.00/child x 60 children x 12 weeks	2,160
T-shirts	
60 x $5.00/T-shirt	300
Transport	
3 trips x $200/trip	600
Locals	3,000
Telephone	
$30.00/month x 3 months	90
Food and Catering	
$3.00/child x 60 children x 60 days	10,800
Insurance 'All-Risks'	1,000
Printing/Photocopying	
$20/week x 12 weeks	240
Total	**$32,590**

Revenues	En dollars US ($)
In kind	
Foundation GTR (proposal)	3,000
Foundation FFS (submission to be made)	8,000
Society BBT (received)	5,000
Foundation ZZC	7,000
Funds collected by YDO	3,130
In nature	
Baptist Church (locals)	3,000
Society TTR (provision)	1,000
Afric-Art (T-shirt)	300
Foods-Plus ($3/child X 60 children X 12 days)	2,160
Total	**$32,590**

5 volunteers will work, each one day a week, free of charge.

11 – Documents enclosed with the submission

- *Tax exemption letter re: 501(c)3 non-profit organization*
- *Board of Directors list of names*
- *Annual Report (or Financial Statements) from previous years*
- *Supporting correspondence from the organizations involved either directly or indirectly into the program or project.*

Describe briefly future program/project(s) susceptible to interest the donor.

Factor 7
Constituents and Transfer
of Know-How
For an organization to run smoothly

1. Taking the first steps to become a constituency

One of the first steps that a foreign organization has to take when desirous to penetrate the American Market is to identify the people who will form a constituency locally and those would be American constituents. Whether your organization is composed of 'natural constituents' or not, it is the duty of an organization, to take the first steps towards enlisting those who may become their constituents. One should not bet on the opposite – no one will come to you to become a constituent. Therefore, it is imperative that you let people know that your organization exists; that they are aware of the existence of your programs or projects and their associated goals.

Near the end of the Second World War, all of the intelligence services around the globe were leading a frenetic race against the clock to trace potential Nazis dissidents. Geneva, the Swiss capital, was the main theatre of this battle in the shadows. At the time every intelligence agent operated in secret under various covers, an American Intelligence Service Agent arrived in the city, rented a sumptuous villa on the main city boulevard and on his door hung a plaque inscribed in gold letters on which one could read: "AMERICAN INTELLIGENCE SERVICE"! When people asked him, not without irony, the reason for this unorthodox behavior in the world of espionage, he gave them a simple answer: "The deserters who are looking for the American protection will know on which door to knock. They will know how to take the appropriate dispositions to enter in contact with me."

This unconventional approach met with success. In a short while, German dignitaries, who could foresee the downfall of the Nazi regime near at hand, were taking appropriate security measures to contact the "American Intelligence Service" Agent at his house in Geneva!

What is the constituency of an NGO?
The constituency of an NGO is an ensemble of persons (physic and moral) who have a common interest or may be involve, in any manner what so ever, with the activities of an organization. The constituency comprises members (past and present) contributors, volunteers, participants, business entities or any one who has similar or complementary interests.

Local Constituency and American Constituency
In order for a foreign NGO to attract successfully charitable funds from America, it needs to build not only a local constituency but an American constituency as well.

The Local Constituency – It is the ensemble of constituents localized in the NGO's country of origin. It will count amongst its members such people as:

- Individuals (members, beneficiaries, leaders, etc.)
- American diplomats living in the NGO's country
- Local corporation
- American citizens living in the country
- Local branches of American organizations (i.e. churches, fraternity, etc.)

- Local subsidiaries of American corporations
- Local communities who share the NGO's historical and cultural values, religious or common interests with foreign communities, (i.e. American of African descent, Asian, Arabic, Jewish, European, etc.)
- Local Foundations and/or foreign organizations established in the NGO's country.
- International institutions established in the country
- Foreign governmental agencies established in the country
- Local institutions and governmental agencies.

The American Constituency – It represents the ensemble of persons who are potential constituents of your organization in the United States.

- Individuals (members, beneficiaries, leaders, etc.)
- Diplomats of your country living in America
- People of your country, region, city living in the United States
- Parent organization which have branches in your country (i.e. churches, fraternity, etc.)
- American corporations which have economic interests in your country
- American communities who share the NGO's historical and cultural values, religious or common interests with foreign communities, (i.e. American of African descent, Asian, Arabic, Jewish, European, etc.)
- American Foundations and/or foreign organizations which have a common sector of activities with your NGO.

To have a huge base of constituents is ideal – however, to ensure success, an organization needs well informed constituents.

Model and composition – The constituency is composed of a series of concentric circles.

- The nucleus comprises members of the Board of Directors, principal donors and management personnel.

- Next, we have the active members, subscribers, beneficiaries, sympathizers, occasional participants, those who have a common interest with the organization and could be potential members and finally the surrounding world.
- Certain organizations such as secondary schools, colleges, universities have natural constituents which comprise their alumni and past student body.
- The community organizations which do not have 'natural constituents.' these NGO's have to build their constituency.

Build the Constituency

Even where 'natural constituency' exists there is a need to build a constituency whilst attracting interest, creating links and initiate the involvement of people into the organization.

The organization must offer to their constituents, opportunities to participate in its programs, to invest in its funding goals and to endorse the values which the organization supports.

Those constituents who are making donations to your organization need to see the impact their contributions have on your programs or projects and merit recognition.

Basis for the Constituency

The constituency can be built on the basis of one or more of the following criteria:

- Emotional
- Professional
- Geographic
- Proximity
- Competitive Spirit

Qualification/Identification of the constituents

The constituents are identified and qualified on the basis of:

- Their link to the organization (originate from same country, professional membership, etc.)

- The interests they have in common with the organization (merchants, politicians, etc.)
- The cause they support
- The size of their wallet
- Their capacity and/or ability to participate in your activities.

Maintaining a Constituency

To maintain an active constituency the organization must

- Evaluate the interests of the constituents
- Honor the donors
- Reward the executives
- Take into account all critics and suggestions
- Encourage feedback
- Maintain an up-to-date address book (database) of the constituents address and coordinates (phone numbers, emails, websites, etc.)
- Establish a telephone network of the constituents
- Keep the constituents informed of the activities of the organization.

Forces which have an impact on the Constituency

The outside (or inside) forces which have an impact on the constituency are:

- Social
- Politic
- Economic
- Ethnic
- Cultural
- Geographic
- Historic heritage (language, colonization, etc.)
- Competition with other organizations sharing the same constituents.

Categories of Constituents

Constituents are divided in eight principal categories

1. Board of Directors
2. Principal donors
3. Personnel
4. Beneficiaries
5. Administrative and political authorities
6. Volunteers
7. Service consultants
8. Sympathizers

Transfer of 'know-how'

Until the beginning of the 18th century, it was known that the death sentence was handed down to any Japanese who went overseas without permission. The man who is considered as the father of rail transport in Japan decided to return to his homeland after an extended sojourn in the United States during which he had the opportunity to learn the technology which put the steam locomotive on its first rails. He was animated of only one goal – that of having his country benefit from what he had learned overseas. Our man was very much aware of the fact that his return to Japan meant death-row for him. Nevertheless his patriotism was stronger than his will to live. Upon his arrival in his homeland, such as the law dictated, he was arrested, put in prison and condemned to death. But he had only one request from His Imperial Majesty before sentence was executed; that of allowing him to build a locomotive and teach rail transport technology to his compatriots before going to the scaffold. After many steps had been taken; demands, requests, and whatever else was required before being granted an audience – he was finally received in court. There, he was asked to demonstrate his 'pretended' technology. He proceeded with an explanation of the 'steam principle' using a boiling teapot which lifted its lid under the force of steam. This demonstration convinced the Imperial Court and our man obtained a stay of execution until he could put in practice what he 'pretended' to be a train, locomotive, railway, etc. After realizing his dream, he was pardoned and elevated to very high functions in the imperial government. Today the rail system in Japan is one of the best in the world. And since that incident, the Japanese citizens traveling the world do not face the death penalty when going home. All of this thanks to the perseverance of one man. It is said that since the Affair of the Japanese Railroad, every Japanese will bring back a piece of technology in his suitcase when he returns home as a token of his symbolic ruefulness for having left his country for a time. Maybe this is one way of explaining the rise of Japanese technology in the modern world.

The constituents are the best craftsmen to transfer technology and know-how to the Third World Countries. In that regard, the Asian people, Chinese and Japanese (in particular) are champions. Actually, there is not one village on this planet which is not represented by one of its native in the United States. Each of these immigrants have learned, however little that may be, something worthwhile.

Factor 8
Lobbyism and Advocacy
The art of influencing those holding the strings of the public purse

The principal role that NGO's play in a society is to propagate thoughts, plead for a cause, influence those holding the strings of the public purse, lift the level of awareness and educate those making decisions and the public at large. The activities of spreading ideas; influence the powers that be, and to lift public awareness can be translated in four categories.

- **'Think-Tank'** dedicated to research, studies, analyses of ideas and propagation of thoughts;
- **Advocacy** to plead the causes of specific and special interests;
- **Lobbyism** to influence the powers that be and those holding the strings of the public purse;
- **Activism** to mobilize, to lift the awareness and to educate the public at large.

We understand by "specific interests" those actions from which the benefits are oriented towards the public. On the other hand, the "special interests" are geared to benefit the members of an organization.

In order to penetrate the American charity, communities need key people to lead the activities in the categories listed above.

'Think-Tank'
The NGO's dedicated to the propagation of ideas among the organizations are called 'think-tanks' – literally meaning a 'vat where the mind can brew and ferment ideas from diverse sources'. The think-tank organizations are dedicated to research programs, studies and analyzing the results which are put at the disposal of the powers that be whether public, diplomatic or other interested parties. The results from these researches, studies or analyses represent a huge opportunity for the NGO's in quest of funding from the donors. They are to be utilized as a data-bank of tools useful to funding applications. The world of think-tank organizations regroups university figures, retired public servants (administration, army, diplomats, corporations, scientists, professionals, etc.)

Activism
Activism can be described as the mobilization, the lifting of awareness and the education of the public on a subject of interest. The activist often doesn't have direct contact with the government representatives but has often an influence on the decision taken by such government administration.

Advocacy
As its name indicates, advocacy consists in defending the interests of someone or in the pleading for a cause given. The aim of most NGO's is to be the advocate for a cause of public (or particular) interest which can be sorted in three (3) categories; information, resources, justice.

a. **Information** – Where the right to have access to information is defended; where formation, awareness and education on subject that have an impact on the quality of life are discussed, upheld and imparted to the public at large. The right to have access to information is generally exercised through seminars, conferences, technical assistance, etc.

b. **Resources** – Where the right of the public to have access to human, financial and material resources necessary to the development of a community is upheld and defended if denied. These services are generally provided through organizations such as the Red Cross, Doctors without Borders, Salvation Army and many religious organizations.

c. **Justice** – Where the public right of the respect for human rights is upheld or defended. These services are generally provided through such organizations as Amnesty International, Committee for the protection of the Journalists, Reporters without Borders, Human Rights Protection Agencies, professional organizations, etc.

Lobbyism

There is very little chance of obtaining anything in the United States if not granted previously according to a law. Therefore, any citizen or group of citizens will be forced, at one point in time, to influence the powers that be to make legislative or regulating decisions upon which a law is to be voted – whereby the 'lobbyism'.

Definition – Lobbyism activities are defined as any communication, oral or written, made with the regulatory body or the government in power, which is destined to influence the decisions taken in regards to any upcoming or changing regulations or laws.

Lobbyism activities are highly regularized and often the subject of controversies due to the fact that they entail money exchange, between the lobbyist and the regulatory body. Any organization benefiting from public support funding is banned from any lobbyism activity. 'Public support funding' refers to any and all organizations benefiting from donations (tax deductible) made by individuals, foundations, corporations, etc.

Lobbyism is directly related, up-stream and down-stream, to the actions of the think-tanks, advocacies and activisms. Therefore, it goes without saying that foreign NGO's need to utilize all the tools at their disposal to find a position in American society – and lobbyism is one of these tools.

The one occupying a public office will not act in function of the interests of a particular organization; he will act in function of his particular political goals – amongst which we find the number of votes, the public opinion, monetary considerations, etc. Of course, monetary consideration is the one form of influence which brings about most controversies.

The exchange of money in the American lobbyism activity rests on a very simple principle. If you give money to an agent of the State in order for him to bypass the law – that's considered as 'corruption'. However, if you give money to one who hold a position in 'legislative body' in order influence him in the process of law making – that's considered as 'lobbyism'.

The origin of lobbyism – There are many versions presented in regards to the origin of lobbyism; the more common being that it first appeared in the corridors of the Parliament in Great Britain circa 1830. Whatever the origin of the term it is undisputable that 'lobby' means 'hall', 'corridor' of an edifice.

For the History buff one has to relate the most widely accepted version of the origin of lobbyism in the United States. Ulysses Simpson Grant, President of the United States between 1869 and 1877 was in the habit of taking a break from his daily routine, in the LOBBY of the Intercontinental Hotel located near the White House. There, the *access* to the President was much easier for the person who had favors or pleas to request from Ulysses Grant. People would come to 'lobby' their cause to the President who now called these people "Lobbyists" (or those people *of* the LOBBY). Thus the term 'lobbyism' would have first appeared in the political vocabulary during the presidential term of Ulysses Grant.

From then on, the term has been used to designate all actions aimed at influencing the powers that be. Despite the fact that some may attribute it a pejorative sense; one could say, that lobbyism is at the base of the American democratic system' success.

The targets of the law

The targets of the law include (but are not limited to) all decisions relating to:

- Preparation or adoption of legislative regulatory measures;
- Granting permits or authorizations of various kinds;
- Granting contracts or subventions;
- Election to public office;
- Various nominations to administrative offices.

Those in Public Office

Those in 'Public Office', considered as targets for all lobbyism activities, are (but not restricted to):

- Senators, deputies, ministers and members of their personnel;
- Personnel members of the government;
- Administrators and personnel of certain governmental organizations or enterprises;
- Some non-profit organization in charge of the management and of the distribution of public funds destined to serve particular projects;
- Elected members and personnel of States' institutions such as the governors, senators and legislature representatives of the States;
- Elected members and personnel of Municipals institutions such as mayors and municipality representatives;

Lobbyism – the engine of democracy

There are two places where one could influence those in public office in their making decisions. *The first* is in the streets or 'underground'. *The second* one is in the halls or corridors of the public offices – thereby the term 'lobbyism' as we have explained earlier.

The first belongs to the authoritarian or dictatorial regimes where the people are cut or disinterested in the process of making decisions of public interest. In this instance only a handful of people think and act in the name of the people. Generally these pretended patriots force the people against those in public office which leads to population uprising, army insurrections and coup-d'états.

The second, the lobbyism belongs to democracies where the people exercise a constructive influence on the powers that be in their daily decision-making process. In a system where the lobbyism is understood and accepted as the rule of the democratic game, each individual, through organizations, is responsible for the defense of its interests. It happens often that the interests of a group are at the opposite end of those of another group. Those who have the best method of persuasion will win. When there is a means to find a compromise, the groups adopt a platform of understanding and, from there, approach those in political office.

The NGO's can do some 'organized' lobbyism directly or indirectly within the limits of the laws in communicating with the people in public office or have recourse to the services of professional lobbyists.

Lobbyism is a legitimate and necessary part of the American political democratic process. Lobbyism is guaranteed as a public right through the First Amendment of the American Constitution which stipulates "The Government will not implement any laws that deals with … **either the right of the people to assemble publicly to address their petitions to the Government in view of redressing their grievances which form the body of their complaints."** (Author's reference)

The freedom of expression, of the press, of association and of lobbyism is the result of the First Amendment. The application of this precept is the strength of the American Democracy. The decisions made by the Government affect together the people and the organizations. Being informed is thus necessary to make an informed decision. The public authorities cannot take equitable and fair decisions without taking into account the information issued from a large base of interested parties. All of the tendencies and implications of any problem must be explored in order to produce a politic of government which is equitable and just.

The *direct lobbyism* consists in meeting with the people in public office to persuade them to take decisions which are safeguarding your interests.

The *indirect lobbyism* consists in influencing the people in public office through community activities such as marches, meetings, open letters, petitions, and telephone calls – all in the name of an organization. The indirect lobbyism is also exercised through the media; press article, editorial, communiqués and through participating in various open debates.

Professional Lobbyists

The preparation and the adoption (or enactment) of a law demands from the lobbyist:

- Research and analyses of the proposed legislations or regulations;
- Monitoring and reporting the findings to the interested parties;
- Educating and persuading the people in public office and their personnel, etc.

In order to defend their cause assiduously and adroitly, and because of the complexity of the process, some organizations may call on the professional lobbyist – however, this requires money.

Different types of lobbyism

Lobbyist Consultant – Any one, earning an income or not, whose occupation or mandate consist in whole or in part, to exercise various lobbyism activities on behalf of a third party, and being remunerated for the consultation work.

Corporate Lobbyist – Any one, whose employment or function within a gainful corporation or company, consist mainly in exercising various lobbyism activities on behalf of the company or corporation which employs him/her.

Organization's Lobbyist – Any one, whose employment or function consist mainly in exercising various lobbyism activities on behalf of an association, a group or organization (gainful or non-profit), the members of which represent several non-profit organizations or are themselves non-profit organizations.

The Occasional Lobbyist – Any one, who exercises a lobbyism activity occasionally, without counterpart, of his own accord or on behalf of a non-profit organization or representing a cause of public interest.

Where do we recruit the 'Occasional Lobbyist'? Constituents and Lobbyism go together. The constituents of an organization are the first soldiers of its lobbyism. Never forget that those who have been elected by the people will fear the people; those who have been nominated to hold a public office will fear public opinion. The constituents have the weapons to ensure that those in public office uphold the laws which should be passed in the interest of the constituency.

What is not considered as 'lobbyism'?
To table in front of those in public office or to make light of the results of impartial research, studies or analyses linked to the goal of an organization is not considered as lobbyism activities.

Who can occupy the post of Professional Lobbyist?
There is no university degrees specifically designed for the preparation in a career in lobbyism. The professional lobbyists are issued from various backgrounds. Most lobbyists have university degrees in political science, journalism, law, communication, public relations, economy, etc. They are often people, who have exercised professions which are in part related to the preparation, the adoption of legislative or regulatory measures and who, for the most part,

have held public office themselves or have been in frequent contact with people holding public office positions. The retired senators, governors, public representatives, members of legislative assemblies, or any retired public office holder can be considered ready to tackle lobbyism activities or been experienced in such matters.

The arguments for and against lobbyism

In his article – 'How to lobby for the Third World', Hans Zamer gives some indications as to the pro and cons of lobbyism.

The arguments 'pro-lobbyism'

- Lobbyism is a constitutional right guaranteed by the First Amendment to the Constitution of the United States.
- The lobbyism uses the democratic paths to obtain the political changes by persuading, reasoning and maintaining dialogue with the powers that be without using force or violence.
- The political contacts with the experts create a forum for opinions and ideas to be expressed and heard.
- The lobbyism allows for open debates to occur outside of the political party spheres of influence.
- The lobbyism is not only the art of persuasion and influence; it is also made of research, studies, scientific analyses which contribute to offer the necessary expertise to the politicians and to clear the tables from demagogic reasoning.
- The lobbyism can redress or adjust the perception of the decision makers and that of the media.
- The lobbyism contributes to validate the laws of the majority whilst taking into consideration the points of view of the minority.

The arguments against lobbyism

- When money becomes the principal mean of argumentation, the lobbyism could validate the points of view of an undesirable minority to the detriment of a majority.
- The decision making process is sometime hidden from the public eye which will thwart the democratic process itself.

- The privileged contacts the lobbyist has with the politicians may become more important than the cause he's defending.
- The professional lobbyist never guarantees results. We must not confuse the lobbyist who can call a senator by his first name with the person who will necessarily have this senator vote in favor of your cause.

Factor 9
Planning Special Events
The management of tomorrow's risks

Definition of a special event – A special event can be defined as any ceremony, manifestation, or organized public gathering such as fairs, festivals, carnivals, expositions, concerts, conferences, conventions, seminars, etc. These are generally designed for the entertainment, the distraction or the relating of information to the public at large. Contrarily to the old adage which says that the one who needs to speak to the Pope goes to Rome, today, the one who needs to speak to the Pope has the option to going to Rome or to inviting the pontiff to his home.

Special events are opportunities to create and reinforce relations between foreign NGO's and those located in America. The foreign NGO's can participate either as guests or as organizers. Hundreds of thousands of special events are organized by the American NGO's annually. One or more of these events without a doubt will respond to the goals and profile of your organization. Where ever you come from on this planet, you will find in the United States, communities and events which represent your race, your culture, your language, ethnic background, nation, religion and historic heritage – or even related to your socio-economic interests or political, professional endeavors can be found in America. The State Fairs and the

Convention Bureaus as well as the Visitors Centers will regroup professionals from tourism and hostelry ready to help you in showing and demonstrating your area of interests. Every State and practically every city has an organism which will facilitate the organization of events such as conventions, conferences, work-shops, seminars, submit-talks, and round-tables, exposition of art objects, carnivals, festivals, parades, concerts, art displays or antiquity showings.

Any organization which is desirous to prosper in the States needs to participate in these special events. A special event gives you the opportunity to organize a fund collection, promotion, and represents the perfect arena for meeting people. The most important perhaps is that a special event will give the opportunity to the donors and volunteers to evaluate the impact their contribution has made on the community (or beneficiaries).

Why a special event?
Certain organizations such as festivals, expositions, fairs, carnivals are special events in themselves. Other organizations will hold special events for various reasons, the best known are listed below.

Reasons to organize a special event
1. Collecting funds
2. Extending the list of donors
3. Recruiting volunteers
4. Sell the organization's image
5. Launch a new program
6. Motivate the principal donors or the members of the Board
7. Distribute information about the organization
8. Collaborate with other organizations to build lasting partnerships
9. Honor the donors
10. Recognize the donors and volunteers' efforts
11. Opportunity to meet the donors and the beneficiaries
12. Utilize the talents and interests of the volunteers
13. Support public interest programs

14. Create emulation between the constituents
15. Engender a détente between all participants, etc.

The five elements which attract media coverage

Millions of events occur every day around the planet. For an event to attract media coverage it must be attractive to the public. Thus, an event must comprise one or more of the following five elements to accede to media coverage – *Celebrity, Conflict, Opportunity, Proximity and the unexpected.*

1) **Celebrity** – Associate an event with the names of dignitaries such as ministers, government figures, presidents, or with celebrities such as sports idols, movie stars, etc. The journalists will run miles to meet a celebrity.

2) **Conflict** – Conflict means 'competitive spirit'. The Olympic Games, World Cups (football, basket ball, hockey, boxing, etc.) are special events built on the basis of un-armed and disciplined conflicts. The success of the 'Sport' resides solely on the competitive spirit it engenders.

3) **Opportunity** – Build your event around historical, cultural and historical facts. The anniversary or centennial celebrations of an historical event may offer the perfect opportunity to organize a special event. For example the centenary of the death of Almany Samory Touré (June 2, 1898 – June 2, 1998) Emperor of Wassoulou in Guinea was the occasion of huge manifestations across that country. You can also build events around cultural displays such as Jazz festival, Movie and Theater Awards or even construct an event on the basis of economic progress such as Auto Expos, Aviation displays, IT development shows etc.

4) **Proximity** – The theory associated with 'proximity' is based on the principle that the public will always be interested in events that occur nearby. The theme of such an event must have a direct impact on the local population. It is in the interest of the local population to have an event which will attract foreign participation. Organize Jazz festival in

Kerouané (Guinea) will not have the same impact on the population as the centennial celebrations of the death of the Emperor did. In Atlanta, where Dr. Martin Luther was born, a multitude of special events are organized to salute the memory of this champion of Human Rights and Non-Violence. Born on January 15th, 1929 and assassinated on April 4th, 1968 in Memphis, Tennessee – ever since 1986 the third Monday of January has been proclaimed by President Ronald Reagan as a National Holiday; the "Martin Luther King, Jr. Day". And since that time Atlanta has been the site of a number of pilgrimages and marches where thousands of people attend the celebrations each year. These comprise, *King-Carter Freedom Peace Walk*); historical tour of the house where he was born (*501 Auburn Avenue*); Prize Award (*Martin Luther King Jr. Community Awards)*; film and music festivals, conferences, etc.

5) **The unexpected** – The unexpected events (mainly those of spiritual value) have often been exploited to build special events around them. Pilgrimages are classic examples of these types of events built around the 'unexpected'. The Fete of the "Lake of Baro" in the Kouroussa Region (Guinea) is well known to attract thousands of pilgrims. It is said that during the festivities the pilgrims' wishes are generally realized. So people go to the "Lake of Baro" Festival to find a solution to their problems expecting a miracle to occur. In the United State the "Crusades" and the "Miracle Cures" assemblies organized by the Evangelists and other spiritual promotional leaders have become common phenomena. These very colorful events attract thousands of faithful and skeptics alike into stadiums and other public arenas. People go to these meetings to be cured of their diseases or afflictions or to see their wishes realized.

The 11 steps towards the success of a special event
1. Select an event which corresponds to the capacity of your organization

a. Name of the event
b. Date of the event
c. Place of the event
2. Think of all the aspects of the event
a. Organization Schedule
b. Number of elements to be considered
c. Contingencies
3. Develop a publicity campaign
4. Select and guide the principal participants
5. Develop a budget
6. Develop a list of the necessary material
7. Planning the work – establish a work plan
a. follow-up, follow-up, and more follow-up
b. Assume nothing
c. Evaluate every detail thoroughly
8. Keep all participants informed on a daily basis
9. Collect all the revenue
10. Honor the volunteers and staff
11. Mix pleasure and 'useful'
a. Define the target amount to be collected
b. Determine the reason for the fund collection
c. Define the manner in which you want to honor the donors, volunteers and participants.

Marketing your events

What is marketing? Marketing are processes followed to plan and develop a series of concepts, sales promotion, and distribution of ideas, goods, and services in order to create trades and exchanges which will satisfy the needs of individuals and organizations.

The '4 P' of marketing

Marketing is based on four essential elements which are; the Product, the Place, the Promotion and the Price – thereby the '4P' of marketing.

Product – The *Product* is what you are offering to the audience and what is valuable to the public. Your product can be a concert, a festival, an exhibition, a seminar any item for public consumption or any other services offered to a community or to the general population.

Place – The *Place* is the site where the event is taking place. The site must be chosen adequately to provide for easy access by public transport or offer car park facility while ensuring that such transport accesses are not miles away from the site of the event. This is important not only for the public attending the event but also for the organizers and participants who have to transport goods (products) to the site. A periodic event and a fixed site are preferable to the choice of a 'road event'. The best method is to fix the dates of the event in regards to the days of the week or the month when it is likely to attract a greater audience. For example, the Indianapolis 500 happens every year on the last Sunday of May in that city. Everyone participating in that event knows where to go and when to be there.

The Space within the Place – The nature of things detests 'empty spaces'. Therefore we suggest never holding an event in a place where you will not be able to fill the space. It is preferable to choose a site where the expected attendance will overflow the premises. A room normally sitting 20 people will appear overcrowded if 30 people attend the event. On the other hand if you choose a room sitting 70 people and only 50 attend, you will give the impression of a meager attendance to your event. Empty spaces during an event denote of failure in the eyes of the observer even if the event drew a greater attendance than expected.

Promotion – The promotion is the means by which you make your product known to the public. Promotion comprises publicity, choice of communication channels, public relations, education and formation of the participants and of the public invited to attend an event.

Price – The price is what you will collect from the audience and interested parties alike, in monetary terms, in return for your product. The price is determined as a function of:

- The value of the event in the eyes of your audience
- The buying power of your public
- The cost of production
- The return on investment or net profit and
- The mode of payment offered to your audience.

The notion of value

The value is the benefit which the audience draws in terms of their needs, availability and pleasure to own a product, or from obtaining a service which is proportional to the price they paid.

The event organizer must know how to put a price-tag on everything that could be of value in the eyes of the interested parties such as sponsorship, publicity windfall (for third party), cost of coverage by the media, access offered to side show stalls (i.e. restaurants, souvenirs shops, etc.).

Risk Management

The major risks that an organizer will face when putting on a show of any kind reside in the losses issued as a result of fire, thefts, vandalism, public brawls or even death by misadventure (i.e. food poisoning). You must remember that any 'unfortunate' incident occurring during an event is the sole responsibility of the organizer unless he (or she) is able to transfer the responsibility onto a tierce person based on 'preventive risk management'. Whether you are an organizer, a guest or a participant in an event, you need to ensure that the risk management option which you have chosen will cover the expenses associated with the losses for which you have assumed the responsibility. Keep in mind that in the United States someone will be ready to sue you for damages at every corner. There are many legal actions taken against tobacco companies whereby the smokers have been awarded millions of dollars because the same company had not warned the smokers of the risks they would run when smoking.

Risk Management Options

When approaching risk management, the first question to be posed is; "What are the probable causes of losses?" The second question is; "What is the cost estimate of the losses?" The potential risks are then evaluated in terms of risk management options such as:

Avoid the risk of interrupting the activities which could engender a source of loss during the event. For example, you can *avoid* the risk of drowning in the river by building a pool in your backyard.

Remember that putting in place a compensation plan for possible internal losses will be beneficial to all parties concerned. For example, some theater owner will demand the payment of a deposit before the event which is destined to cover the damages done to his premises (i.e. broken furniture, vandalism, etc.)

Control the risk with safety and security programs put in place before the event which will ensure a reduction of the loss. This type of risk can be controlled in different ways – for example, ensure that none of the guests or participants to a show enters the premises with any type of arms or blades. Another option which is regularly chosen by exhibition and expo organizers is the enrolment of security guards to patrol the premises during, before and after the show – thus preventing (as much as possible) vandalism and thefts.

Transfer the risk to a third party or to the insurance company. The majority of risks can be covered by insurance contracts or ensuring that a third party has done so *before* the event.

Whether you participate in an event in the United States or whether you invite Americans to participate in a event in your country, you must ensure that all risks (as far as foreseeable) are covered and that all responsibilities are clearly delineated and on whose shoulders they may rest.

Factor 10
Leadership and the decision making process
Transform a problem into an opportunity

Something to think about when it comes to leadership

Nine leaders in ten have succeeded in their enterprises thanks to what they have learned at their own expenses. The tenth one is probably born with a silver spoon in his mouth!

You are rarely said to be 'a-born-leader' – usually you are thought to be a leader.

The world is not looking for a leader who has done good deeds, but for a leader who can choose to accomplish great deeds.

The risks in the profession of leadership

Man are not reasonable, they are illogic, and egotistical
Love them anyway

If you are a Good Samaritan, many may say that you were
motivated by personal interest
Be a Good Samaritan anyway

When you succeed, you will attract untrue friends and true enemies
Fight to succeed anyway

The good things you do today will be forgotten tomorrow
Do good things anyway

Honesty and truthfulness are making of you a vulnerable man
Be honest and truthful anyway

What takes years to build can be destroyed from one day to the
next
Be a builder of good fortune anyway

I.   What is a leader?

There is no universal definition for the word 'leader'. One of the
'down-to-earth' definitions would be: a person who takes the lead.
For me, I consider as a leader, **the one who has the courage to
transform his problems into opportunities for his fellow-men.**

A leader must be able to 'lead' the men under him and possess
a specific talent which inspires others to follow him. The quality of
a leader of men and the specific talent vary according to the goal of
an organization.

Leadership qualities

A leader must possess the following qualities:

1.   **Honesty** – Being honest in his conduct and in the application
     of the decisions and regulations adopted by the organization.
     There cannot be imbalance of power in good leadership.
2.   **Commitment** – Personal commitment is the first quality in
     good leadership behavior. Commitment is the quality which
     allows to opening the door to all other qualities which the

leader needs to attain his objective. A leader must be able to say; 'Since someone has to do it, might as well be me'.

3. **Trust in your men** – Trusting someone is to be able to tell him that he is capable to do something and to give him something which he is capable of doing. Men will give their life for a cause when a leader will make them understand that they are capable of undertaking the task ahead. Every man has an incredible amount of inner energy ready to be ignited the moment someone trusts him. Controlling someone's work is not controlling the person doing the job and it is not a sign of lack of trust; but it is assuming one's responsibility. A good leader must ensure that the task undertaken by one or another has been accomplished to the satisfaction of all concerned. If that doesn't happen, no one will care about what they do – if no one is there to appreciate the man's work.

4. **The talent to listen** – To know how to listen and how to draw the appropriate conclusions from what you have heard is a talent. Information is power. A leader must listen to all of the people in order to identify the problems and give the appropriate answers or the means to remedy such problems. There is always a time to listen and a time to act.

A good listener must
*   Give his undivided attention to his interlocutor
*   Let the interlocutor express his ideas entirely and let him go to the end of his reasoning.

A good listener must not
*   Be busy doing something else whilst his interlocutor is speaking (i.e. watch TV during a conversation).
*   Be ready to interrupt his interlocutor at every turn.

The six steps to listen effectively
*   **Be attentive** – Be ready to listen attentively to what the person has to say.
*   **Be physically receptive to the messages** – The voice of the speaker is generally audible, so the listener must show that

he is physically receptive to what is said.

- **Select and organize the material** – To insure the message is well received (if you are the speaker); the material you are offering to the listener must be well organized and you must help the audience to comprehend the message using images, graphics, microphones, etc.
- **Interpret the communication** – The listener and the speaker must communicate in the same language, thus using the language of the audience will help your listener in the interpretation of your message.
- **Response** – The listener will assist the speaker from time to time in finding the right word to say. It is important to show the interest you have in what is said.
- **Memorize** – The good listener will be able to memorize what has been said during the conversation and will thus be able to follow the reasoning of his interlocutor.

5. **Diplomacy** – Using force to resolve a problem must be of last resort. The leader must use diplomacy and persuasive avenues before resorting to force.

6. **Recruiting talent** – One of the qualities shown by a good leader is his ability to breaking a large project into small manageable pieces and to find the right people to assume the tasks and responsibilities attached to each piece. The results will be positive if the objectives are clearly defined and if the efforts are satisfactory and well rewarded. Listen to the people to know what personal satisfaction they will draw from their work.

Some advices relevant to the leadership of men
- Practice evaluation – give positive feedback for individual performance
- Practice 'role-reversal' – give people different responsibilities and educate them in assuming different roles
- Use internal talents to teach others new trades or practices
- Ask everyone to fix their goal and evaluate them according to these goals.

7. **Assuming a positive attitude** – The leader must always assume a positive attitude which will attract trust in his judgment, promote humility, respect of others, tolerance, but will also advertise firmness in his commitment and in his decisions.

8. **Self confidence – Be obstinate in attaining the assigned objectives.** At the base of any master piece, you will always find the obsession of one man in the belief that his project was feasible from the beginning. Nothing is worse than a leader who changes his goal at every turn.

9. **Be able to fix his objective** – One of the main function of a leader is to be able to focus the effort of his organization towards one and sole objective.

II. Different kinds of leaders

There are two sorts of leaders; the 'task leader' and the 'maintenance leader'. Every organization needs leaders who have these qualities.

a. Task Leader – The task leaders are the ones who know how to 'get the job done. They're generally very good in situations such as these:
- Prepare the day's agenda
- Recommend the objectives to be reached
- Determine the key questions
- Suggesting the paths to follow in order to accomplish a specific task in due time
- Clarify all data input
- Record the information and subsequent decisions

b. Maintenance leader – The maintenance leaders are people who have the knack for being at the right place at the right time and who have the talent to reinforce the emotional and cohesive behavior of the people in the organization. That kind of leader is the moral support of anyone involved in any given project. They're generally involved in the following circumstances:

- Welcoming and introducing people
- Listening attentively to any idea tabled by others
- Involving everyone in the discussion
- Encouraging all the shy people to express themselves
- Thanking people
- Giving positive feedback.

However, in the real world, people who possess all of these qualities at once are not found at every street-corner. The world is not looking for a leader who has done good deeds, but for a leader who can choose to accomplish great deeds. The leadership talent can be developed.

III. Making decision
The greatest responsibility for a leader is to make decisions. To take an appropriate decision at the appropriate time, the leader must be guided by his intuition, lean on the talent of others and/or count on the collaboration of everyone – given the circumstances.

There are three manners in which a decision can be taken: executive, consultative and collaborative.

When a leader makes a decision based on his intuition, the decision is said to be *executive*.

When a leader makes a decision based on the experience and capability of someone else, the decision is said to be *consultative*.

Lastly, when a leader makes a decision based on the common opinion of his colleagues or assistants, the decision is said to be *collaborative*.

In a democratic society this is what is described as the 'the three branches of power'; **The Executive Power**, in the person of the President of the Republic or the Head of Government; **The Consultative Power**, symbolized by jurisprudence (Supreme Court); and **The Collaborative Power** personified by the parliamentary body of government (i.e. senators, deputes, governors, etc.)

How to determine the best way to take a decision

Each organization must define within its articles or internal statutes and regulations the manner in which a decision should be taken by all constituents.

1. Executive Decision

The leader makes decisions, based on his knowledge and prerogatives.

The executive decision is appropriate when time is of the essence.

- The problem and the solution can be clearly defined
- The decision does not necessitate a change in value, attitude, or creed amongst the constituents
- The leader had the expertise and prerogatives necessary to make the decision alone.

Example: The toner cartridge in the photocopy machine is empty! It is not necessary to consult a specialist, or call a meeting of the Board to decide whether or not (or how) to buy a new cartridge – the model and reference number (and price) of the item are well known, and to obtain a new cartridge only requires a phone call.

2. Consultative Decision

The leader, in this instance, will seek advice from specialists such as a lawyer, a doctor, an accountant, (or anyone who has useful information on the subject) in order to resolve a particular problem.

The consultative decision is appropriate when time is *not* of the essence.

- The constituents and/or participants can be seriously affected by the decision
- The constituents have the necessary expertise to resolve the problem
- The problem is real but the solution is unclear
- The leader has analyzed the problem within the limits of his competence but is not prepared to lose some of his authority

through making the wrong decision.

Example: The organization has decided to buy a new computer. The leader will call on a technician seeking his advice as to the choice of computer which will respond to the needs of his organization – make, model, speed, capacity, etc.

3. Collaborative Decision

The leader and the constituents will decide together on the best course of action to resolve a particular problem. In this instance the leader's vote will not weigh heavier than anyone else in the organization.

The collaborative decision is appropriate to make when;

- There is enough time to meet and table the problem
- The creed, value or attitude of the constituents must change in order to resolve the problem
- The problem and let alone the solution, are not well defined
- The expertise or experience of many must be taken into consideration
- The leader and the constituents are reasonable enough to accept the responsibility and share the consequences of the decision.

Example: The organization needs a more powerful and more versatile computer to replace the 'ancient' model, which no longer responds to the needs of the organization – but the coffers are empty! The purchase of a new computer will necessitate supplementary contributions from the constituents. In this instance, the advice of a technician is necessary to clarify and explain why a new computer is needed. The advice of each of the members is necessary to ensure that they are prepared to make the sacrifice and participate in the purchase of the new piece of equipment. Meanwhile the organization will continue to use the old machine.

Note: In any case, the leader retains the responsibility for making the final decision.

IV. Conducting a meeting and tabling the agenda

- Begin and end a meeting in due time as per schedule
- Develop an agenda and follow it rigorously
- Focus the discussion on the points listed on the agenda
- Maintain an atmosphere conducive to the participation of the members
- Re-cap the principal points or decisions taken periodically
- Maintain a record-of-minutes of the meeting regarding the decision that have been adopted during the meeting
- Identify (clearly) the tasks to be undertaken
- Confirm the responsibilities of each individual concerned
- Consider the agenda for the next meeting – proposed date/ time

How to face dissidence

- Do your homework
- Identify allies and opposition
- Request that each one registers
- Request that those people who wish to speak register
- Request that the questions be written down and tabled officially (preferably in advance of the meeting)
- Do not allow a non-member to address the meeting
- Limit the time for each speech
- Limit the discussion to one subject per person
- Do not allow for the distribution of leaflets or any materiel which has not been previously reviewed and accepted by the Board
- Know your mission, and remain steadfast in your commitment
- Listen attentively and try finding common ground of understanding or compromise
- Select a person to speak on your behalf or on behalf of the Board as the case requires.

Factor 11
The Board of Directors
The legal proprietor of an organization

I. Rights and Obligations

One of the important tasks of a NGO is the configuration of its Board of Directors. According to the law, an organization is the exclusive property of the Board of Director. The manner in which the Board exercises that right and assumes its obligations of proprietor are defined by the laws of the country (or the State) in which the organization is established and by the regulations and statutes inherent to that organization. An organization is considered as a moral entity represented by the Directors of the Board. An organization therefore, enjoys all the privileges of an individual. Amongst these prerogative statutory rights the Board of Director has the power to:

- Suing or being sued according to the judicial process of the land;
- Complain or defend the name of the organization;
- Possess and affix the seal of the organization;
- Acquire, purchase, rent, keep, use, own chattels in the name of the organization and engage in any and all real estate transactions;
- Elaborate, negotiate, sign and execute any form of contractual

agreements and assume the responsibilities thereof;
- Elect and appoint members and officers of the organization;
- Establish, modify, amend its statutes and its regulations;
- Borrow money within the framework and for reasons inherent to the well being of the organization;
- Possess and exercise all powers necessary and useful to execute all activities linked directly or indirectly to the object for which the organization has been created.

In most States, the minimum age to accede to a Board of Directors' position is 18 years old.

Legal responsibilities of the Board of Directors

Under the dispositions established by laws and regulating the activities of the non-profit organizations (NGO) the members of the Board must observe certain codes of conduct, maintain standards and obey a variety of regulations in the execution of their responsibilities towards the organization. The codes of conduct are generally described as '*obligation of care, loyalty and obedience*'. Most States have laws (which may vary from State to State) that will define the obligations, rights and responsibilities of the members of the Boards described under the headings cited above. These laws will be applied during judicial procedures to determine whether or not a Board member has acted properly in the course of his functions.

Obligation of Care

The *Obligation of Care* describes the level of competence expected of a member of the Board, which is commonly expressed as: "the care an ordinary person would have taken whilst occupying a similar position and under similar circumstances". That means that the member of the Board has the obligation to exercise his functions with *vigilance* and *prudence* particularly when making decisions within the framework of the activities of the organization and affecting its participants or constituents.

Obligation of Loyalty

The *Obligation of Loyalty* is the fidelity principle which is adopted by each member of the Board within the organization towards the legal, administrative or judicial precepts, to which he has sworn allegiance at the time he became a member of that Board. Consequently, each Board member must renew his allegiance to the precepts named above and to the organization every time he makes a decision which affects the organization. That means that a Board member may never use the information he has been privileged to obtain in that position to personal ends. He must always act in the best interest of the organization.

Obligation of Obedience

The *Obligation of Obedience* recommends that the members of the Board demonstrate the will to attain the common goal of the organization. The Board members must be equally *obedient* to the laws and regulations intern or extern to the organization. They are not allowed to act in a manner which is not consistent with the objective of the organization. The basis for this rule of conduct goes hand in hand with the trust the people will demonstrate in the organization and in its ability to carry out its obligations in regards to the funds donated and in the execution of its mission.

Number of Directors in the Board

The number of Directors sitting on the Board is determined by the needs of the organization. If the essential role of the Board is to establish a set of rules and regulations which will be carried out by qualified personnel within the organization – the Board does not need to comprise many members. However, some Board of Directors need a greater number of seats to be filled in view of assuming the responsibilities of raising funds and to execute organizations' programs.

The number of members sitting on the Board needs to be defined in the statutes of the organization. One of the techniques used to determine the number of Board members initially is to fix a minimum and a maximum number of members (e.g. from 5 to 25 members), so that the number could be increased in due course in accordance with the expressed needs of the organization. Using this method a Board can add a member to its rank without having to modify its statutes.

Term of the mandate for a Director (or Officer) of the Board

The term of the mandate needs to be determined and included in the statutes of the organization. The ideal method is to fix the term to three years or six years, and to have a third of the members renew their term every year or every two years accordingly. This system allows for the Board to ensure a continuity of membership to the Board. Some organizations have renewable mandate at term.

Election

Most organizations which do not have a 'membership' (or constituency) have a selection committee in charge of electing new Directors. The organizations which have a membership base have 'general elections' that invite all members' participation in the election of new Member.

The Board of Directors

The Board of Directors is composed of two kinds of members: The Officers and the Directors.

The Officers

The Officers represent the *executive body* of the organization. They execute the decisions taken by the Board and report to the Directors on their activities.

The Officers are:
- The President
- The Vice-President
- The Treasurer
- The Secretary

Note: The organization can elect more than one Vice-President, Treasurer or Secretary.

The Directors – Legislative Power

The Directors participate in the decision making process and control the execution of these decisions by the officers and staff. In other terms they form the *Legislative Power* of the organization.

II. Individual responsibilities of the Board Members

Each member of the Board has a personal responsibility.

- Attend all Board meetings, all committee meetings and be on attendance to all special events.
- Be informed and keep informed of the mission, services, and the overall politic of the organization and its inherent programs.
- Review the agenda, and all references to be cited, prior to each Board meetings or committee meetings.
- Serve in at least one of the executive committee and assume a specific task.
- Make a personal financial contribution to the organization.
- Inform the public of the organization's activities.
- Suggest the recruiting of at least one person susceptible to bring additional resources (monetary or talent) to the organization.
- Keep up-to-date with the situation/position of the organization.
- Follow the direction concerning conflict of interests (if need be) and maintain the general political position of the organization confidential.
- Abstain from making undue requests from the staff.
- Assist the Board in the maintenance of its fiduciary responsibilities such as the review of the Annual Report and/or Financial Statements.

The personal characteristics of the members

The members' personal characteristics to be taken into consideration are, amongst others;

- **Competency** – The competence to listen, to analyze and to think clearly and in a creative manner; work hard and assiduously with the persons or group of persons involved in all organization's activities.

- **Will Power** – The will-power to be prepared to attend the Board and committee meetings; ask the right questions, assume the responsibilities and follow-up on the execution of the decisions made by the Board. Make substantial financial contributions according to the circumstances, be open to suggestions made by the committees or by the Board and be willing to evaluate one-self.

- **Will Power** – Be prepared to develop certain talents such as fund raising, recruiting members and volunteers. Read and understand the financial reports. Learn more about the programs of the organization.

- **Possess** – Possess the tolerance necessary to accept the views of others which may be contrary to one's own opinions. Be honest. Have a team-player spirit, maintain a friendly approach, and be patient as well as responsible for one's actions. Have the talent to be (or become) a community builder; have personal integrity, a sense of value, be concerned with the development of one's organization and most importantly – have a *good sense of humor!*

The diversity of the Board of Directors

The composition of the Board of Director must reflect the diverse communities which it will serve. The elements to be taken into account are:

- **Competency** – Certain member of the Board need to have knowledge in management, law and accounting.
- **Age** – It is important to have members of the Board that represent every age group in the community.
- **Race and religion** – The races, ethnicity and religions of a community must be represented by the Board members.
- **Background** – It is advantageous to have members of the Board which are issued from various backgrounds; private sector, government, or having experience in other NGO's.
- **Services users** – Most organizations have people associated

to the Board who are representing various social sectors which are served by the organizations' programs.

III. The responsibilities of the Board of Directors

The members of the Board assume the following responsibilities:

Personnel – The Board has the responsibility to;
- Engage the personnel (staff) employed by the organization,
- Write their 'work-description' and list their obligations,
- Approve the regulations which govern the staff's activities,
- Control the execution of their tasks,
- Evaluate their performance,
- Reward their devotion and/or 'a job-well-done'.

Finance
- The Board approves the budget of the organization,
- The members ensure that all expenditures are included in the budget approved by the Board,
- They ensure that expenditure reports are submitted regularly to the Board.

Fund Raising
- All requests for funding must be submitted to the Board for approval prior to being presented to the funding source.
- The Board needs to approve all plans related to special fund raising campaigns.
- All members of the Board need to participate in fund raising campaigns.

Planning
- The members of the Board must approve all long or short term programs or projects designed by the organization.
- It is also necessary for the Board to oversee the execution of the program/project according to the approved plans.

Public Relation

The members of the board must be kept informed as to all of the organization's activities in order to better promote the efforts, enhance the results and improve (or maintain) the image of the organization.

The Board's responsibilities

The Board as a moral entity is responsible for:

1. Giving direction

- Develop and maintain the focus onto the mission of the organization and onto its goal.
- Establish and supervise the strategic directives of the organization.
- Fix the political objectives of the organization.
- Delegate the management powers of the organization.
- Express, safeguard and promote the values of the organization.

2. Ensuring the resources

- Identify the human and financial resources necessary to the execution of the mission of the organization.
- Establish an acquisition politic of these resources, inclusive of those concerning the participation of the Board members.

3. Ensuring supervision

- Establish a politic of financing and fix the responsibilities.
- Ensure the maintenance of professional ethics and the observance of the laws.
- Follow up on the progress and on the evaluation of the objectives to be attained.

4. Acting as an Appellate Court

- The Board of Directors must act as an *Appellate Court* in the resolution of personal problems – only in case of *force majeur*. The application of rigorous internal regulations and of a process of review of complaints should reduce considerably the risk of conflicts and frictions amongst the members of staff.

The ten responsibilities at the basis of a Board of Directors

It is important to enumerate once again the responsibilities befalling the Board of Directors of an organization.

1. Determine the mission and objectives of the organization,
2. Select the executives,
3. Support the executives,
4. Ensure effective planning of the organization's activities,
5. Provide adequate resources to the organization,
6. Manage the resources effectively,
7. Determine, delineate and supervise the programs and services offered by the organization,
8. Improve (or maintain) the organization's image,
9. Serve as an Appellate Court,
10. Evaluate one's own performance.

The Committees

In order to provide efficiency in the execution of the chosen actions or programs, the Board of Directors, may choose to create committees which will assist and counsel the Board members in specific fields of activities. The committees are composed of members and non-members of the Board.

The number of committees created by the Board of Directors depends largely on the programs and services offered by the organization. It depends also on the number of Board members and the availability of volunteers.

The most common committees are; the finance committees, cultural committees, conflict resolution committees, special events organization committees, etc.

The Executive Committee

The Executive Committee is created in view to facilitate the decision making process concerning routine activities which do not necessitate a sitting of the Board. This method is used mostly in the case where the Board comprises a plethora of members which convenes only periodically (i.e. every quarter or every year).

The members of the Executive Committee are generally chosen amongst the officers sitting on the Board of Directors. Directors may be appointed as members of the Executive Committee according to the Board's wishes. In any case only Board members sit in the Executive Committee.

IV. Roles and responsibilities of the Officers

President:
The president has the responsibility to:

- Supervise and control the affairs of the organization.
- Supervise and control the activities of the officers and staff.
- Preside over all meetings of the Board and General Assembly of the members.
- Execute the Titles.
- Sign the contracts, checks and all other documents necessary and useful to the good management of the organization.
- In general, the President must execute all tasks that are assigned to him/her; determine and observe the statutes and regulations inherent to the organization.

Vice-President:
The Vice-President will assume interim function and the continuation of all of the organization's activities in the absence of the President.

Secretary:
The tasks of the Secretary are to:

- Keep originals and copies of the statutes and regulations inherent to the organization up-to-date.
- Maintain files of the organization's records, the list of members, the minutes of the Board and Committee meetings as well as the minutes of the General Assembly meetings.
- Notify all members of the dates and venue of the meetings
- Keep the seal and records of the organizations.
- In general, execute all the tasks that are assigned to him/her

by law, observing the statutes and regulations inherent to the organization.

Treasurer:

The Treasurer is the:

- Custodian responsible for the safekeeping of all funds and valuables owned by the organization.
- He/she is the person depositing the funds and values into the banks or into other financial institutions designated by the Board.
- He/she is the recipient and the signatory to the receipt of all funds or values entering the organization as well as being responsible for all accounts payable by the organization.
- He/she will effect all payments.
- He/she is responsible for the keeping of all accounting books and records of the organization – reporting on debits, credits, losses, profits and all other financial transactions of the organization.

V. The formation cycle of a Board of Directors

Phase 1: Identification – Identify the human resources need of the Board in terms of competency, talent, knowledge, contacts, etc., and in terms of what is necessary in order to execute effectively and profitably the strategic plan of the organization.

Phase 2: Cultivate relations – Cultivate the relations with the members of the Board. Invite the current and past members to contact and to raise the interest of those potential members in the activities of the organizations.

Phase 3: Recruiting – Recruit the potential resources personnel – It is important at the outset to know what to expect from the future Board member (i.e. financial resources, competency, connections, etc.). Explain to the future member what is expected of him. Never minimize the responsibilities nor diminish the tasks that may be associated with the position. Incite participation.

Phase 4: Orientation – Orientate the new members of the Board as to:

The organization; narrate the history of the organization, describe the programs, challenges, financial status, internal statutes and regulations and give the incumbent an organizational chart.

The Board of Directors; describe the committees, the members responsibilities, the tasks assigned to each of the current members, and give the incumbent a list of the members of the Board, members of staff and key people in the organization.

Phase 5: Engagement – Engage all members of the Board according to their competency and availability. Involve the members of the Board into the committees or assign specific tasks. Ask for feedback in order for everyone to remain accountable for the work to which he/she has been assigned. Express your appreciation for 'a job-well-done.'

Phase 6: Education – Educate the Board. Provide the members with necessary information (brochures, publications, clippings, documentaries, etc.) related to the activities of the organization. Promote the study and analyses of the problems facing the organization. Go to 'retreats'; organize outings and encourage the members to participate into development activities such as seminars, work-shops, conferences, etc... (Again, don't hide the difficulties facing the organization.)

Phase 7: Rotation – Rotate the members of the Board. Take into account the performance of each of the members before renewing their mandate (or not). Encourage the 'low performance' members or those who are not readily available to yield their seat to new people. Develop new leaders.

Phase 8: Evaluation – Evaluate the Board's performance as a whole and individually. Encourage each member to make a self-evaluation. Take a census regarding the means and approaches to use in order to improve performance.

Phase 9: Celebration – Celebrate victories and progresses as small as they may be. Appreciate individual contributions made to the Board or to the community. Leave space for good humor and joy of living particularly in times of crisis.

VI. Characteristics of the Board of Directors

There are many sorts of the Board of Directors – the Board with the following characteristics would be best to avoid.

1. Board 'New Start'
Major characteristics

- Once elected, the Board member receives little or no formation or orientation.
- The President is often elected (by abstention) without adequate description of what is expected of him/her – nor given clarification as to his responsibilities or obligations.
- The officers of the organization are not familiar with their role or their responsibilities.
- The role and responsibilities of the Board of Directors and/ or of the staff are not clearly defined.

2. 'Counselors' Board
Major characteristics

- Just a few members sit on the Board
- The quorum is usually (or often) attained by telephone conversation.
- Most of the Board members have the same backgrounds.
- Some of the committees are made up of only one member.
- The committees called 'Roulette' where each member sits on other committees are common occurrences.
- Members who disappear without a trace is a natural phenomenon.

3. 'Parrot' Board
Major characteristics

- "We've already done that and it doesn't work."
- "I don't know anyone."
- "I thought you were doing this job."
- "You must have voted on this while I was away…"
- "He never does anything."
- "What do you want me to do?"
- "I didn't know I was going to do this…"
- "I didn't have this information when I gave my consent."
- "We must hire someone to do that."
- "It won't work…"
- "Whoever does this, usually, is away."

Are amongst many others the excuses used by such of Board.

4. Board 'Relax'
Major characteristics

- The members of the Board have little or no sense of responsibility or obligation.
- Very few members are engaged in specific tasks or projects.
- The members have very little or no contact with the clients and participants.
- The members of the Board and the members of staff would not recognize each other if they met in the street.
- Most of the members don't know what is expected of them.

5. 'Dear Leader' Board
Major characteristics

- The founder of the organization becomes President Omnipotent – Director, Executive who is probably an excellent visionary but not necessarily a good administrator.
- The members of the Board as well as the staff only consult the 'Dear Leader' for everything.

- A large variety of the programs respond only to the available resources and not to the mission of the organization.
- The Board and the staff are more preoccupied with satisfying the 'Dear Leader' than they are to attain the organization's goal.
- The committees are formed for appearances only because all decisions reside with the President (the Dear Leader) anyway.
- The Executive Director often acts as President of the Board.

6. 'Deep-pockets' Board
Major characteristics

- The members of the Board are recruited according to their wallet size.
- There are very few committees (other than financial) which are functional.
- The absenteeism at Board meetings is very high.
- The members of the Board rarely represent the community which the organization is supposed to serve.

7. 'Busy' Board
Major characteristics

- The members of the Board are more preoccupied with drawing some profit from their participation in the activities of the organization than they are of serving the interest of the organization and they are often engaged in operations that result in conflict of interest.
- The members do not attend the Board meetings regularly.
- The members make no effort to keep informed of the important problems that the organization may face from time to time in the course of its activities.
- The administration system is not efficient and does not ensure the legal and appropriate operation of the organization.
- The Board members often sit on other Boards of organizations which are as inefficient as any other.

8. 'Phantom' Board

Major characteristics

- The Board meets rarely or only meets for occasions such as marriages, funerals or baptism of a member's family.
- There are different people sitting at each Board meeting.
- The introduction and chit-chats take more time than the meeting itself.
- The quorum is rarely attained.
- The members are badly informed or receive made-up information which they don't take time to study.
- The debates are stretched out of time because no one is prepared to confront the situation facing the organization.
- The Board called "Geographic Phantom" comprises members residing around the globe.
- Only the executive committees meet regularly (more or less) and ensure the leadership of the entire organization.

9. 'Microscopic' Board

Major characteristics

- The major portion of the time is dedicated to finding solution to problems not specifically related to the organization. There is always a specialist missing in the group which has to be *found* someplace else.
- The major part of the meeting is dedicated to identifying the problems and not to finding solutions.
- The formations are to no end, and do not offer a positive result or improvement to the running of programs or activities.
- "If we only knew..." is the popular phrase used during the meetings.
- The pleasant outings are frequent – to supposedly solidify the relations between members; whilst the Board remains *non-operational* and the members remain good friends.

10. 'Assembly-line' Board

Major characteristics

- Most, if not all members of the Board, have the same backgrounds or their experience and expertise are similar.
- All the members, or nearly all, are providing services from other organizations.
- Most Board members are also members of staff.
- Most Board members are also clients (or beneficiaries) of the organization.

Factor 12
The first legal document
The Articles (record of the minutes) of the constituency

The *Articles* or the "Minutes of the First Organizational Meeting" is the first legal document (as opposed to the statutes and internal regulations) and it is the most important document of your constituency. This document demonstrate the will of two (2) or more people to unite their material, financial, intellectual, and moral resources (etc.) in order to attain a common goal. That goal could be charitable, commercial, political, cultural, scientific, educational, etc. The Record of Minutes must be precise and succinct.

The "Minutes of the First Organizational Meeting" (and the Articles therein) of the general assembly of an organization is the document on which rests all the acts of an organization. Contrarily to the other documents, once the contents of the Articles have been adopted (voted upon); the Record of Minutes describing the Articles of the organization cannot be modified, erased, changed or amended. This document is unique and has a historical value for the organization and anyone associated with it. To be a signatory of the First Record of Minutes of the general assembly of your organization can confer immortality to your achievements.

The Articles of the organization must cover, among other things, the following points:

1. Names of participants;
2. The object of the meeting;
3. The individual or collective consent of the persons attending the meeting (or those absent) to adhere to the object of the meeting;
4. Determine the positions to be occupied by officers;
5. Elect the officers;
6. Select the Directors;
7. Choose the name of the organization;
8. The postal address of the organization;
9. Whether or not to 'incorporate' the organization;
10. Nominate the Agents who will be responsible for the incorporation of the organization;
11. Preparation for elaborating the statutes (Bylaws) and regulations of the organization;
12. Tax exemption according to Section 501(c)3 of the Fiscal Code;
13. The goal to be attained (or maintained) by the organization;
14. Type of exemption from which the organization will benefit;
15. General discussion regarding the 'orientation' of the organization;
16. Date and venue of the next meeting – "The Last Word"; date and signatures.

The legality of the internal statutes and regulations of the organization

As we have mentioned earlier, it is important to note that according to the laws of most States, the "BYLAWS" (Statutes) and "REGULATIONS" of an organization are not considered as legal documents. These documents are working tools and references proper to the organization. It is thus important for the statutes and regulations of your organization to be conform to the laws of the

State in which your organization is incorporated. Any statute or regulation in opposition to the laws in force will be considered null-and-void. Therefore, any organization must take care to adopt statutes and regulations which conform with the laws of the State. Once the Articles are adopted their applications must be strictly respected by all members. Consequently, you must be prepared to introduce clauses to the Articles, statutes or regulations which allow for their modifications in case of necessity due to changing circumstances or in case of emergency. The process, by which these modifications may be elaborated or put in place, should not be an easy task. Again, the statutes and regulations are the fundamental tools of the organization. They are essential if not indispensable to the harmonious relations between all members of an organization.

Elements to be considered when establishing the "bylaws" (statutes)

1. Name of the organization;
2. Object of the organization (i.e. charitable, educative, advocacy, development, etc.);
3. Members' qualifications:
    *   Voting or non-voting members
    *   Condition of eligibility.

4. Meetings of the members (not to be confused with the meetings of the Board);
    *   Venue, date, interval;
    *   Means of notification of the meetings (i.e. letters, telephone, messages, etc.);
    *   Elements to be mentioned in the notification;
    *   Definition of the quorum – number of members that must attend the meeting (generally 2/3 of members or the majority of members should be attending general assembly meetings).

5. The Board of Directors
    - Process of nominating and electing members of the Board;
    - Qualifications required of a Director and of an Officer;
    - Term of mandates;
    - Resignation, vacant posts, demotion, suspension of membership.

6. The meetings of the Board of Directors
    - Presiding the meetings;
    - Venue and interval of meetings;
    - Quorum.

7. The Officers
    - Responsibilities and duties;
    - Nominations of President, Treasurer, Secretary and Directors.

8. The committees – Permanent committees
    - Qualifications of committee members;
    - Role and responsibilities of the committees.

9. Articles; and maintenance of the Records of Minutes and all financial records.
10. The fiscal year – start and end of a fiscal year
11. Contracts, checks, etc.
12. Distribution of assets in case of organization dissolution
13. Amendments and modifications of the statutes/regulations.

Write the statutes in a language common to all people and avoid complicated terminology.

EXAMPLE

Articles of Constitution for the Organization
"Actions and Community Services, Inc."

This example describes the essential elements which need to be addressed in the Articles of the organization.

Step One – Name of the Participants

Register the names of the persons attending the Constituency Meeting. In most States, the formation of an organization necessitates the membership of a minimum of three (3) people. You must ensure that the minimum number of members required by the law of the State, or country, where you wish to incorporate your organization, is observed.

> Example: *We, the signatories of the present Articles of Constituency, attending the meeting on this 27th day of January 20__ called to order to constitute a non-profit organization in accordance to the laws of the State of (Indiana), which are regulating the activities of non-profit organizations, have recorded that:*

> *The following people were present at this first constituency meeting: Ottokar Cisse, Veronica Bingoo, Velomoto Sylla, Motovelo Camara, Jean Woddra, Mamadou Djankee, Bineta Tarah, Pierre Attakuru, Emile Tonfice, and Boubakar Anlevor.*

Step Two – Describe the object of the meeting

First general assembly meeting called in order to establishing a non-profit organization

> Example: *This meeting is the first general assembly meeting called by the members in order to create a non-profit organization which will be established and will conduct its*

activities under (and observing) the laws that regulate the non-profit organizations in the State of (Indiana).

Step Three – The individual or collective consent of the persons attending the meeting (or those absent) to adhere to the object of the meeting

Make particular mention of the persons attending the meeting which will be members of the Board. In order to establish a charitable organization (with non-adherent membership) it is suggested that the Board limits its membership to five people. A Board membership of five (5) to seven (7) people allows for additional resource membership at a later date.

> <u>Example:</u> *All the people in attendance such as listed above have consented to be members of the Board of Directors of this organization.*

Step Four – Designate the posts of officers of the organization (i.e. President, Vice-President, Treasurer and Secretary)

> <u>Example:</u> *The second item on the agenda was the identification of the posts of officers of the organization. The Board had designated the following posts of officers of this organization; which will be – a President, a Vice-President, a Secretary and a Treasurer.*

Step Five – Select or elect the people who will fill the posts of officers of the organization.

> <u>Example:</u> *The Board has selected the following people to serve as first time officers of the organization:*
> - *President : Ottokar Cisse*
> - *Vice-President : Veronica Bingoo*
> - *Secretary : Velomoto Sylla*
> - *Treasurer: Motovelo Camara*

Step Six – Selecting the Directors

> <u>Example:</u> *The Board has selected the following people*

to serve as Directors of the organization: Jean Woddra,
Mamadou Djankee, Bineta Tarah, Pierre Attakuru, Emile
Tonfice, and Boubakar Anlevor

Step Seven – Choose the name of the organization

The law calls for the name of an organization to include one
of the following terms (or its abbreviated form) – Corporation,
Incorporated, Company, Limited.

> Example: *The discussion then addressed the subject of the*
> *choice of name for the organization. The Board has adopted*
> *the following name to be the name of the organization:*
> ***"Actions and Community Services Inc."*** *This name will*
> *be used on all non-legal (e.g. letterhead, business cards,*
> *etc.); all legal documents, forms and tax returns required*
> *documentation.*

Step Eight – The organization address

Choose the address of the organization. It is suggested to opt for
a Post Office Box (at the post office) to avoid having to change the
organization's address every time the address of one of the founding
members changes.

> Example: *The choice of the organization's official address*
> *was then tabled. It was decided to take a postal box to ensure*
> *permanency. This formality had been completed prior to the*
> *meeting and the address of the organization is now: P.O. Box*
> *007, Indianapolis, IN, 46000, USA.*

Step Nine – Whether or not to 'incorporate' the organization

The Board must decide whether to formalize (or not) the
establishment of the organization. Incorporating an organization will
legitimize its existence and will allow it to operate freely on various
level of governmental or non-governmental related activities. The
incorporation also allows for the separation of responsibilities and
risks thereof. There are two principles behind the incorporation of a
company (or organization).

a) The Board members of a corporation are not responsible for the actions or the debts incurred by the corporation;

b) The incorporation establishes the organization as a legal entity and facilitates its relations with other organizations, legal entities, societies, government agencies, etc.

Example: *The subject of whether or not to incorporate the organization was tabled and debated. The Board has decided that the organization should be incorporated and bearing the same name as chosen above.*

Step Ten – the Incorporating Agents

If you decide to incorporate the organization, then there is a need for nominating the persons who will be in charge of the incorporation of the organization on behalf of the members.

Example: *Next, the Board decided that Messrs...will be the in charge of incorporating the organization and will execute all formalities other than those required by the Secretary of State in order to duly and formally incorporate the organization.*

Step Eleven – the elaboration of the statutes

Establish and erect the bases on which to develop the internal statutes and regulations of the organization.

Example: *The attention of the Board then focused on the elaboration of the bylaws (internal statutes) of the organization. The following people; Jean Woddra, Mamadou Djankee, Bineta Tarah were assigned to draft the statutes of the organization.*

Step Twelve – Tax exemption according to the fiscal code – Section 501(c)3

Determine the section of the Revenue Code under which the organization should be functioning. There are several types of non-profit organization which are classified under Section 501(c).

The most advantageous is perhaps Section 501(c)3. (See 'Types of Exemptions' – Factor 1.)

> Example: *The Board has decided that the organization will be a 'Public Charity' organization established under Section 501(c) of the Revenue Code of the Internal Revenue Services.*

Step Thirteen – The Object (goal) of the organization
Define the object or goal to be attained by the organization.

> Example: *The organization was formed in order to reinforce and improve the prevalent capacity of the community groups. The first activities will encompass leadership and management formation of the members and the establishment of humanitarian contacts in view of developing the communities and improving their activities and services.*

Step Fourteen – What type of exemption?
Define the type of exemption from which the organization will benefit. There are over thirty (30) types of organizations which are exempt from paying taxes.

> Example: *The motion was tabled and passed that the organization will be recognized as a entity exempt of taxation according to Section 501(c)3 of the Revenue Code of the Internal Revenue Services.*

Step Fifteen – General discussion surrounding the subject of the 'orientation' of the organization

> Example: *The ensuing discussions surrounded the subject of the necessary future actions and activities of the organization.*

Step Sixteen – Next meeting
Don't forget to determine the:

- Date and time of the next meeting
- And (most importantly) remind everyone *where* the next

meeting is to be held.

Example: *The next meeting of the Board will be on March 25th, 20... at 4:00pm to be held at the public library.*

Step Seventeen – 'The Last Word' before adjourning the meeting

Example: *The meeting was successfully concluded at 6:00pm on this _____ day of _____ 20... and was thus adjourned.*

Step Eighteen – Date of the meeting
Date, month and year at which the meeting was held.

Example: *Dated on this 27th day of January 20...*

Step Nineteen – Signatures
Names of the signatories to the documents and their signature

The law requires for three (3) people to sign the Articles of the organizations.

1) *Signature_____ Name _____*
2) *Signature_____ Name _____*
3) *Signature_____ Name _____*

MODEL OF THE RECORD OF MINUTES

Articles of the Constituency Meeting
"Actions and Community Services Inc."

page 1

We, the signatories of the present Articles of Constituency, attending the meeting on this 27th day of January 20... called to order to constitute a non-profit organization in accordance to the laws of the State of (Indiana), which are regulating the activities of non-profit organizations, have recorded that:

The following people were present at this first constituency meeting: Ottokar Cisse, Veronica Bingoo, Velomoto Sylla, Motovelo Camara, Jean Woddra, Mamadou Djankee, Bineta Tarah, Pierre Attakuru, Emile Tonfice, and Boubakar Anlevor.

This meeting is the first general assembly meeting called by the members in order to create a non-profit organization which will be established and will conduct its activities under (and observing) the laws that regulate the non-profit organizations in the State of (Indiana).

All the people in attendance such as listed above have consented to be members of the Board of Directors of this organization.

The second item on the agenda was the identification of the posts of officers of the organization. The Board had designated the following posts of officers of this organization; which will be – a President, a Vice-President, a Secretary and a Treasurer.

The Board has selected the following people to serve as first time officers of the organization:
- *President : Ottokar Cisse*
- *Vice-President : Veronica Bingoo*
- *Secretary : Velomoto Sylla*
- *Treasurer: Motovelo Camara*

The Board has selected the following people to serve as Directors of the organization: Jean Woddra, Mamadou Djankee, Bineta Tarah, Pierre Attakuru, Emile Tonfice, and Boubakar Anlevor

The discussion then addressed the subject of the choice of name for the organization. The Board has adopted the following name to be the name of the organization: "Actions and Community Services Inc." This name will be used on all non-legal (e.g. letterhead, business cards, etc.); all legal documents, forms and tax returns required documentation.

The choice of the organization's official address was then tabled. It was decided to take a postal box to ensure permanency. This formality had been completed prior to the meeting and the address of the organization is now: P.O. Box 007, Indianapolis, IN, 46000, USA.

The subject of whether or not to incorporate the organization was tabled and debated. The Board has decided that the organization should be incorporated and bearing the same name as chosen above.

Next, the Board decided that Messrs...will be the in charge of incorporating the organization and will execute all formalities other than those required by the Secretary of State in order to duly and formally incorporate the organization.

The attention of the Board then focused on the elaboration of the Bylaws (internal statutes) of the organization. The following people; Jean Woddra, Mamadou Djankee, Bineta Tarah were assigned to draft the statutes of the organization.

The Board has decided that the organization will be a 'Public Charity' organization established under Section 501(c) of the Revenue Code of the Internal Revenue Services.

The organization was formed in order to reinforce and improve the prevalent capacity of the community groups. The first activities will encompass leadership and management formation of the members and the establishment of humanitarian contacts in view of developing the communities and improving their activities and services.

The motion was tabled and passed that the organization will be recognized as a entity exempt of taxation according to Section 501(c)3 of the Revenue Code of the Internal Revenue Services.

The ensuing discussions surrounded the subject of the necessary future actions and activities of the organization.

The next meeting of the Board will be on March 25th, 20... at 4:00pm to be held at the public library.

The meeting was adjourned at 6:00pm

Dated on this 27th day of January 20...

*Signature*_____ *Name* _____

*Signature*_____ *Name* _____

*Signature*_____ *Name* _____

Factor 13
America and its four fundamental declarations
Independence, Power, Rights and Duty

At the corner of Martin Luther King, Jr. and 12th Streets, in Indianapolis you can find the 'Crispus Attuck' Middle School. If, the name of the Martin Luther King Jr. is familiar to my reader that of Crispus Attuck is less known to most people. Yet, Crispus Attuck, as unknown as he is, is the man whom History has recorded as the first martyr in the battle of Independence. Fallen under the fire of the British soldiers during the riots which led to the Independence of the thirteen colonies, Crispus Attuck was different inasmuch as he was *black*. Descendent of slaves, he knew what *freedom* meant to men. If History remembers Crispus Attuck particularly among so many who were killed on that day in Boston, and everywhere during the events that followed, it is certainly due in part to the fact that he was a black man. What difference would the death of one black man make to the conditions of life for the black people at that time, which would justify the ultimate sacrifice made by Crispus Attuck? Posed in that manner, the question would bring you to answer: "Nothing much that would justify dying for it." However, Crispus Attuck believed in freedom and he joined the ranks of the combatants because he firmly believed in the principles highlighted in the Declaration of

Independence of the thirteen colonies which was signed in congress on July 4th 1776 in Philadelphia. The principle most sacred in the heart of many stipulates that: *"We hold these truths to be self-evident, that all men are created equal, that they are endowed by their Creator with certain unalienable Rights; that among these are Life, Liberty and the pursuit of Happiness"*

In order to understand the works of the American Society, we invite the leaders of the Non Governmental Organizations to read some of the texts related to the founding of American institutions. Among these texts we will cite four of the most important ones:

- **The Declaration of Independence**
- **The Declaration of Power – The Constitution** (issued during the Convention of Philadelphia)
- **The Declaration of Rights** – (The Ten First Amendments to the Constitution and some that follow)
- **The Declaration of Duties – (The laws** and decisions of the courts and tribunals).

I. The Declaration of Independence

The Declaration of Independence is the first document signed unanimously in congress, by the representatives of the thirteen American British Colonies, in Philadelphia on July 4th 1776. This document is an enumeration of fundamental principles, reasons for the separation from the British Commonwealth and grievances against King George III of England.

Fundamental Principles – The fundamental principle put in evidence concerns the equality and the rights of all men. They were eloquently expressed in the following terms: *"We hold these truths to be self-evident, that all men are created equal, that they are endowed by their Creator with certain unalienable Rights; that among these are Life, Liberty and the pursuit of Happiness"*. Today 'Liberty' and 'Equality' remain very dear to the American man. But liberty and equality are not things that are acquired on a daily basis.

It is an eternal combat; because the liberty of each of us stops where that of others begins. In their fight for survival, men are constantly competing to surpass and dominate others. Once freedom was acquired, the Americans didn't stay idle; they continuously fight to preserve their 'liberty'. This principle is at the base of so many other texts amongst which is found the "Ten Amendments to the Constitution", better known under the name of "Bill of Rights" (or Declaration of Rights) and the other amendments which comprises the abolishment of slavery and all of the laws concerning the rights of men.

Another principle recommended in the Declaration of Independence is 'Prudence'. Prudence is recommended regarding the change of government for 'light or transient causes'. *"Prudence, indeed, will dictate that Governments long established should not be changed for light and transient causes…"*

To avoid the consequences brought about by a change of government for 'light or transient' causes, the Constitution elaborates upon the following precautions:

"Immediately after they shall be assembled in consequence of the first election, they shall be divided as equally as may be into three classes. The seats of the Senators of the first class shall be vacated at the expiration of the second year, of the second class at the expiration of the fourth year, and the third class at the expiration of the sixth year, so that one third may be chosen every second year; … "

This, in fact, allows for a continuity of government in the Senate as well as preventing new comers, from their sheer numbers, to shake or dismantle the established order of governmental powers.

The grievances against King George III were many. However, we can remember one thing; the delegates to the Convention destined to elaborate the Constitution of the United States had forgotten certain grievances addressing the individual rights of the citizens;

which error was later rectified through the adoption of the first Ten Amendments to the Constitution.

II. The Constitution of the United States of America
(or the Declaration of Power)

The Constitution issued from the Convention of Philadelphia was signed on Monday September 17th, 1787. It was ratified by the Legislative Assembly of the former thirteen colonies and was put in force in 1789, some thirteen years after the Declaration of Independence. Today the United States of America counts fifty States under its banner and several territories and 'possessions', in addition to Washington D.C., the Capital which doesn't belong to any State, Territory or Possession. The Constitution of the United States of America is the fundamental law of that country – it constitutes the basis of all American institutions.

As wise as those we call affectionately the "Founding Fathers" were, the delegates to the Constituency Convention have called the Constitution, the "Declaration of Powers", in comparison with the first Ten Amendments known under the name of "Declaration of Rights" – or "Bill of Rights". In fact, if the Constitution issued from the Convention of Philadelphia is quite explicit regarding the 'powers of government' distributed in three branches (*Executive, Legislative* and *Judiciary*), it is silent in regards to the Rights of the Citizens of the Land; which error would be corrected later with the issue of the first Ten Amendments.

Beware of the People
From the minutes taken during the debates, it appears that the Founding Fathers were leery of the People; or more precisely, they were wary of these "pretended patriots". For some (if not to say all) of the Founding Fathers to be wary of the People, they had to have good reasons to be so. Some delegates, such as Sherman of Connecticut, thought that the People should not be preoccupied with the matters of government. *"They are ill informed,"* he said. *"They*

are continually exposed to the unknown to the point of erring." Such statement would seem absurd today especially coming from a leader of government which is purporting to be *"...of the people, by the people and for the people"*. However the People of America were never to regret the sagacity of their Founding Fathers in this regard.

Gerry, of Massachusetts, had better reasons yet to be leery of the People. The crisis that had followed the war had forced a great number of the citizens of his State to ask for the Legislative Assembly's assistance in resolving the problem. However, the help had never been forthcoming and the population had intervened at the Supreme Court level – fully armed and demanding resolutions whilst attempting to take-over the United States Arsenal at Springfield. Although the insurrection of Shays had been swiftly repressed and the people put under control in February of 1786, Gerry was in no mood a year later, to have the People accede to power – or have any say in the matter either. *"The People do not aspire to virtuous endeavors,"* he declared in front of the Delegates at the Convention. *"It is a dupe of false patriots."* And when talking about the remunerations granted to civil servants, he added: *"It seems that it is the motto of Democracy to leave the civil servants to die of hunger."*

Secret Deliberations

The taste for keeping secrets among the Founding Fathers began with the elaboration of the Constitution. The decision of the Delegates was that all debates be held in absolute secrecy. The participants swore not to let anything leak from their discussions. The press was kept at bay. It was prohibited for the Delegates to talk about what went on indoors outside of the meeting rooms. Even the drapes had been drawn closed to avoid indiscreet gases.

In fact, the Convention itself adopted a 'rule of secrecy' to be maintained throughout the deliberations. No copies of what was written in the records of the deliberations, during the sessions, could be made without the authorization of the *Chamber*. The members could only consult the records on site and could not copy its content for later review. Nothing that was said during the meetings of the Assembly could be printed, published or communicated in any manner whatsoever, without the authorization of the convening members. When Thomas Jefferson, in Paris, learned of this decision, he regretted that the delegates had marred their deliberations with such an 'abomination' without precedent and in so doing had tied their tongues.

The argument in favor of secret deliberations – If in fact the Delegates didn't want to be tied to their prime opinions, not firmly established, they wanted even less to be responsible for false hopes or vanishing dreams that the publicity surrounding their discussions could ignite in the hearts of the People. Before temporary decisions were to be made public in the State of Georgia or in New Hampshire, they would have had time to be modified in Philadelphia where the Convention was held. Antagonism issued from erroneous decisions, reported late in the day, could very well persist without regard for the final results. Also, some could feel obliged to support the proposals of their delegates and oppose those made by rival States. Above all, the Delegates at the Convention wished to be judged for their achievements when presented as a whole and not in part. In fact, most decisions were adopted by consensus, concessions, or compromises. The Delegates took into account the preoccupations, worries and moods of each and everyone; big and small States, pro-slavery and anti-slavery supporters, populated States and under-populated States, monarchists, and those in support of the Republic, rich and not-so-rich States, Federalists, and Confederates, etc.

In a letter addressed to a friend in Virginia, Washington wrote: *"To please everyone would be impossible, attempting to do so would be in vain. That is why the only path to follow in the construction of such that, after all of the opinions have been expressed and that all of the circumstances of the moment have been considered, the customs, etc, etc; it could withstand the scrutiny and critics and that it could inspire confidence of its good sense and for the People to put it in practice. The demagogues, the men who are not disposed to lose anything from what forms the States, will be opposed to any general government. But one could not consider them with much concern while justice, one must hope, will prevail with time."*

It is in this atmosphere of suspicion towards the People, and armed of sagacity that the Delegate elaborated the Constitution of the United States. As we have made mention earlier, the Delegates faced a dilemma; create a weak government would lead to anarchy, create a strong central government could allow for the emergence of a dictatorship. Jefferson feared that the Presidency created by the new constitution may endanger the Republic.

In a letter to Lafayette who shared Jefferson's concerns, Washington explained: *"In my judgment, there couldn't be any danger that the President, by means of intrigue, could not maintain his position, even less that the post remain so, if it is not in the case of abasement to the lowest kind of morality or of the worst sort of political depravation. And even if it were the case, there are as many other dangers looming for another form of domination to prevail. When the People have become incapable of governing themselves they are ready to be subjected to the power of a master and it is of no consequence from where ever this master would emerge."*

Therefore, there was a need to establish a power that was neither weak in regards to the security it had to represent, nor strong for the safeguard of the liberty it guaranteed. In front of such dilemma, in the eyes of the Delegates, the solution was not in the intervention of the People in the affairs of government. Such government needed to find a solution by itself. But, as we will see later on, the solution came in fact from the powers given to the People in the first Ten Amendments to the Constitution.

The Constitution or the "Declaration of Powers"

Placed in context with the preceding document – the Declaration of Independence, and in regards to the Bill of Rights, as well as taking into account the spirit which animated the Delegates of the Convention, the American Constitution, looked at closely; it resembles a true Declaration of Powers... of the Government. Consequently, as a constitution designed for a democratic society, it was not perfect. But as a basic document, it was the best that could be produced by human minds to avoid the possible insertion of tyrannical powers into the government. Governor Morris of Pennsylvania, in view of supporting the establishment of a supreme and strong government, noted that the Government of the States and the Federal Government could not be considered all at once as a supreme governing power, inasmuch as 'supremacy' with more than one head is unconceivable – there should be a sole governing body or none at all. "*It would be better for us to admit to a supreme government as of now, than having to bow our heads in front of a despot later; because the despot will rise amid the anarchy that may result from the actual confusion.*"

Some factors eventually spun the wheel of fortune in favor of the establishment of government "humanly perfect".

- The Delegates at the Convention did not have to submit to the authority in power at the time. Their only masters were the people of the Legislative Assembly in each of the State they represented.
- Neither the Delegates, nor the States which they represented, were obliged to adhere to the Constitution, if the People of the State, didn't not consent to do so freely.
- At that stage, there wasn't any consequence if some State decided not to adhere to the Union. There wasn't any risk of being branded as secessionists. The only risk was that the State could not count on any future assistance from the Union in case of aggression from outside and even less in the case of troubles brewing within its boundaries.
- The risk of being isolated in case of non adhesion to the Union was a very influential factor motivating the Delegates to attain a constructive consensus – It was evident that the Old Master, Great Britain, waiting in the wings to re-establish power in some of the newer States was a risk not to be taken lightly.
- Most concerns pivoted around the fact that the Delegates wanted their respective State to maintain their *freedom*. They

were worried to lose their liberty in favor of a central, supreme power. However they were also extremely conscious of a liberty being acquired without being conferred the protection it demanded.

- The States were at liberty to adhere to the Union at the time of their choosing.

The Articles of the Constitution

The Constitution is composed of; a Preamble, seven (7) Articles which comprise twenty-four (24) Sections. The Preamble starts with: **"We, the People of the United States..."**

The First Article comprises **10 Sections** – It confers the legislative power to a Congress which contains two Chambers; the Senate and the Chamber of the Representatives.

The Second Article comprises **4 Sections** – It confers the executive powers to a President of the United States of America.

The Third Article comprises **3 Sections** – It confers the judicial powers to the Supreme Court and to other courts instituted by the Congress (First Article).

The Fourth Article comprises **4 Sections** – It defines the rapports between each of the States; between the State and its citizens and between the federal government and the States.

The Fifth Article comprises **1 Section** – It determines the conditions and procedures to follow in order to amend the Constitution.

The Sixth Article comprises **1 Section** – It re-affirms the treaties, debts and engagements taken by the States under the Confederation. It imposes to all government agents to swear allegiance or to assert to defend the Constitution of the United States.

The Seventh Article comprises **1 Sections** – which describes the conditions of ratification of the Constitution by each of the States.

To create a 'balance of government' the Constitution established three branches of government: Executive, Legislative and Judicial.

If these three branches of government allow for the creation of equilibrium within government, they do not guarantee an equilibrium between government and its constituents.

The Three Branches of Government

The Executive Branch (President)

The Executives Powers are conferred to the President of the United States. The President is elected for a four year term. The Executive Branch of the government is thus represented by the President. He is the Chief Executive Officer in charge of the operations of the Federal Government. He is not elected by universal direct vote such as is the case in France, for example. The President is elected by a system of electoral wards. Each State disposes of a number of electorates equal to the number of Senators and Representatives who represent those States in Congress. Each State has two Senators and a number of representatives proportional to the population of that State. Today there is one elected representative for each 300,000 people. At the beginning there was one representative for each 30,000 people. Therefore a candidate could win universal votes although loosing the election – which was the case of Al Gore in 2000; when he had almost 400,000 votes over those of George Bush. But, when the 'electoral count' came through, Bush had won the election.

As we have mentioned earlier, the Founding Fathers were leery of the People and were conscious of the eventual 'slippage' at the issue of popular elections. Therefore the President has "VETO" Power.

The Legislative Branch; the Congress (the Senate and Chamber of Representatives)

All legislative powers granted by the Constitution are conferred to the Congress of the United States. The Congress is composed of two chambers; the Senate and the Chamber of Representatives.

The Senators – Each State disposes of two Senators elected for six years. Today they are elected by universal votes, which was not the case at the origin of the Constitution. In fact, the President and the Senators were then chosen by the legislative assembly of each of the States. This disposition was abrogated by the passing of the 17th Amendment on April 8th 1913, or 126 years after the ratification of the Constitution in 1787 in Philadelphia. The People were then sufficiently 'mature' and 'educated' in political matters to be able to choose their Senators – one supposes that to be the case...

The Representatives – commonly called the 'Congressmen' or 'Congresswomen', they are elected for two years by universal and direct votes from the people of each State which they represent – thereby the term of 'Representative'. They are the representatives who are supposed to represent the people of the State at the Federal Government Levels. Their number is proportional to the population of their State.

The Judicial Branch – The Supreme Court and Lower Courts

The Judicial power is conferred to the Supreme Court and to the Lower Courts such as the Congress deems it appropriate. The judges of the Supreme Court and of the Lower Courts will remain in position for as long as they are worthy to receive their salary and for as long as they are not demoted in their functions for whatever reason. The precedents set by the courts have the power of law, and will remain in force for as long as they are not superceded or cancelled by a superior court.

Slavery

The most virulent discussions surrounding the subject of slavery were dealing with the matter of importation of slaves into the United States. The Constitution does not mention the word "slave" anywhere in its content. Martin of Maryland raised his voice against slavery saying: *"Slavery is incompatible with the principles of the revolution and it would be dishonorable for the American character to have the Constitution marked of such a word."*

Masson of Virginia added that slavery was the enemy of progress. *"The people demean the work when it is accomplished by slaves."* And went on to say: *"Slavery attracts judgment from Heaven on the Land. Since nations cannot be recompensed or punished in the here-after, they must be on earth. Because of an ineluctable succession from cause to effect, Providence will punish the national sins with national calamities."*

The Constitution therefore, treats of the problem of slavery in other terms. Those terms are more economical than racial. It speaks of 'free men' or of 'other men' – meaning the slaves.

The States

In the image of the Federal State, each State has its own Constitution and its own government which also comprises three branches.

1. Executive – conferred to a Governor and to the Lieutenant Governor, elected;
2. Legislative – the legislature of some States comprises two Chambers: The Senate and the Chamber of Representatives. In other States, the legislature comprises only one Chamber.
3. Judicial – conferred to a Supreme Court of each of the States.

Prerogatives of the Federal Government

Some of the prerogatives afforded by the Federal Government can be listed as follows:

*   United Postal Services
*   Diplomatic – the relations between the United States and other Governments in foreign soils.
*   Declaration of War or Rebellion – such as during the War of Secession.

- Immigration – and all the rules and regulations attached thereto are governed by the Federal Government
- Money – Many countries have tried to beat the American Dollars but none have had much success...
- The Laws governing the States must be conformed to the Spirit of the Constitution of the United States.

The Secret Lodges

Contrarily to what some of the Founding Fathers thought, the American People demonstrated that it had a definite sagacity; wise enough in fact to demand for the Bill of Rights to be included into the Constitution and the sagacity to abide by these rights and precepts which included not to involve itself with the matters of Government. When the Bill of Rights was adopted as integral part of the Constitution, some leaders were alarmed at the idea that the People were now able to take part in the affairs of government. Thus, they took upon themselves, using the 'freedom of association' as their backdrop, to fend off some malevolent intent which could ensue from a too wide exposure of the public affairs to the public... Hence, they decided to discuss some of the important 'public matters' during more or less 'secret' meetings (away from the 'public eye'). Such secret lodges as the Free Mason are said to have been establish at that time.

It is said (behind close-doors) that George Washington, the First President, was to ascend to the Imperial Throne of the United States contrarily to the Spirit of the Constitution. But George Washington was sufficiently wise to decline the offer from the Free Masons.

III. The Declaration of Rights and other Amendments

One would be tempted to think that the United States owes its democratic success to the plurality of its political parties. In reality, the American democracy rests on the dynamism of its constituency. The Constitution of the United States doesn't make reference to the direct role played by the political parties in the life of the country.

The political parties, such as every other form of organization which are not related to the cog-wheels of the government, owe their legitimacy to the famous First Amendment to the Constitution.

The First Ten Amendments are called the "Bill of Rights" (or Declaration of Right). They were ratified on December 15th, 1791; four years after the elaboration of the Constitution of 1787. If we may consider the original Constitution as the affirmation of the *powers of government*, the First Ten Amendment must be considered as the affirmation of the *Rights of the People.*

The First Amendment stipulates:
"Congress shall make no law respecting an establishment of religion, or prohibiting the free exercise thereof; or abridging the freedom of speech, or of the press; or the right of the people peaceably to assemble, and to petition the government for a redress of grievances. "

It is this amendment which delineated the powers granted to the People. These powers allow the People to counterbalance the powers attributed to the three branches of government by the original Constitution. From the spirit in which this amendment was written, were issued the five branches of the constituency directly related to the five fundamental rights:

1. Freedom of Religion
2. Freedom of the Economy
3. Freedom of Press
4. Freedom of Association (NGO)
5. Political Freedom.

1. Freedom of Religion
Freedom of Religion cannot be effective without tolerance and respect of the religious beliefs and philosophies of others. The colonials who landed in America were in majority people who had escaped persecution on the basis of religious beliefs. That is why they were called "Pilgrims". They were fleeing an England of which the Crown had contributed to the establishment of an 'official religion'.

Freedom of religious practice and of laicism of the Government of the United States have become, today, so sacred, that one could say that they are as sacred (if not more so) than religion itself.

2. Freedom of Economy

The debacle of the communist regimes has demonstrated that the Freedom of Enterprise is the best form of economy which guarantees freedom in the pursuit of happiness. One of the Delegates at the Convention illustrated the value of a sound economy in any society in these terms: *"Life and liberty are maybe, in the first instance, dear to savages, but property is the first design which a civilized society shall pursue."*

One of the positive aspects of free enterprise is that it favors the plurality of expression, the creation of multiple enterprises and press institutions, which in turn, guarantee the freedom of speech. As we have mentioned earlier, the Press is before all an economic activity.

3. Freedom of Press

The Press is all together an economic activity and an intellectual product. It is often considered as the symbol for the freedom of expression, although we are not always at liberty to say whatever passes through our brain, or publishing it in whatever media. The paradox is even more flagrant when considering that the Press organ in a democratic society is the one institution where speech is the most restrained. Economic exigencies, philosophies and sometimes political pressures are the brakes applied to the freedom of expression in the Editor's office.

Asserting that the Press constitutes the "Fourth Power" is debatable. There is no 'Fourth Power'; in fact there are only two powers: the power of government embodied in the three branches of the Executive, Legislative and Judicial powers and the Constituency Power embodied by the People distributed into five branches – political, economic, religious, press, and associations (NGO). The perfect example of these powers at work is the one of the poor fellow who found himself thrown in prison because he thought he confided in a friend when he gently criticized Saddam Hussein in front of him!

These five forms of liberty cannot be affirmed if not conditional upon the Freedom of Speech. Freedom of Speech, by itself, has no significance if not exercised in relation with the five types of freedom. Moreover, these liberties have no power if not exercised within the framework of associations.

4. Freedom of Association (NGO)

The four other branches of the Constituency cannot be validated if they are not practiced within the framework of associative power. The will of the People to defend its particular interests through non political, laic or non-profit organization, is the first guarantee of democratic freedom. These organizations (or associations) are best known under the name of "Non-Governmental Organizations" or NGO's. Every time, in the course of History, that the people have found themselves in a situation such that they were forced to hand their problems over to political, religious or economic powers to defend or satisfy their particular interests (other than political, religious or economic), they always fell into the yoke of tyranny – thereby losing all other fundamental freedom and rights, without obtaining those they sought.

Despite their respect for politics, their devotion for religion, their esteem for economic pursuit, and their attachment to the Press, the American People has been sufficiently wise, until now, not to fall under the charm of the politicians, religious leaders, employers and other journalists to defend their particular interests. The equilibrium afforded between the four other branches of the Constituency provides for a solid counter-weight to the three branches of Government.

A more in depth observation brings us to the conclusion that the dynamism of the NGO's has become the 'guard-dog' of American Democracy. This is in direct opposition to the popular belief that the Press is the 'Guard-dog of Democracy'.

Since we know that in a democratic society, the government must not have any State Religion, nor have any State Corporation, nor control the Press direction, or even less impose a unique political party to the People, one could conclude that any non-political organization would be branded a 'Non Government Organization'. But the term is used to mean something else. In the United States, what is commonly called a NGO elsewhere; will be called a "not-for-profit organization" or better known yet as a "Non-Profit Organization".

5. Political Freedom

As in all democracies deserving of the name, the government of the United States has no official party. In fact, the Constitution makes no reference to political parties whatsoever. The legitimacy of the political parties is issued from the First Amendment to the Constitution – within the clause mentioning that the People have the right to assemble in peace and present their grievances to the government, etc. The object of the political parties is to control the branches of government through elections processes and through the nomination of those assuming public functions. Therefore, the political parties have ambiguous positions; they are, at times, government representatives (when everything goes well) or, at other times, they are constituents (when Lady Luck is not on their side); yet they are sometimes saddling over both functions (when they try to please everyone).

The American political system is dominated by two major party representations; 'The Republicans' and 'The Democrats'. There are also two or three other parties said to be 'Independents' who represent the 'Greenies' or those unhappy souls, or even those that have been *abandoned* by the major parties. The American political parties are unique in that they have no national leaders such as it is the case in other countries. The party is a simple electoral machine which is not linked or associated to anyone or anything. The elections held within the parties are designed to choose candidates to elect those in public functions rather than to choose a party leader. The odds have no structural ideology. The ideological doctrines are carried through two major channels; the 'Conservatives' and the 'Liberals'. The majority of Conservatives are Republicans whilst the Liberals are for the most part Democrats – but their affinity to the parties stops there. The ideological movement means 'big businesses' and 'big money'. They make the think-tank organizations and the media editorialists very happy indeed. Whether a candidate supports conservative or liberal principles, he will be consequently upheld in its beliefs by the editorialists and ideologists on either side of the board.

The reason, for which there are no national parties, but rather national committees of party representatives, is simple. Since no one is allowed to regularize without restraining; any attempt to regulate the associations (political, religious, etc.) would have to be considered as a form of restriction of freedom – which is prohibited by the First Amendment to the Constitution. Thus, all regulations related to any form of associations are the responsibility of the State. Each State has its own laws and regulations concerning the legislation and the functioning of any organized associations. The laws of each State will apply only to those organizations which are incorporated in that State; an organization incorporated in one State will be considered as a 'stranger' in another State where it is not incorporated. (See Factor 1) Consequently, the national party structures are only a gathering of political parties which are functioning independently from one another. The political parties function literally as franchises would. They lend their name to local structures which they use as banners in the same fashion as thousands of franchises use the MacDonald banner across the world.

Other Amendments in the Declaration of Rights

The debate surrounding the First Ten Amendments to the Constitution is without end. We never talk enough about it. So, to keep with the form, we are going to discuss (very briefly) a few aspects of these amendments.

The Second Amendment – guarantees *the right of the people to keep and bear arms*. Therefore it is not surprising to note that the American Police Officer has a 'finger on the trigger'. This amendment is 'guarded territory' of the very powerful organization "National Riffles Association (NRA)". This organization counts nearly ten million members; it is very active and financially very solid. It goes without saying that it watches carefully for this amendment not to be modified or altered in any way.

The Fourth Amendment – guarantees *"The right of the people to be secure in their persons, houses, papers, and effects, against unreasonable searches and seizures, shall not be violated, and no warrants shall issue, but upon probable cause, supported by oath or affirmation, and particularly describing the place to be searched, and the persons or things to be seized".*

The Fifth Amendment – guarantees that a citizen *"shall be compelled in any criminal case to be a witness against himself, nor be deprived of life, liberty, or property, without due process of law..."* In other words it belongs to the prosecution to give proof and show evidence as to the culpability of the accused. This amendment gave rise to the famous Miranda versus Arizona from which is issued the not less famous 'MIRANDA WARNING'. (See Factor 1)

The Fifth Amendment – also guarantees that *"shall any person be subject for the same offense to be twice put in jeopardy of life or limb..."* – Meaning that no one can be judged twice for the same crime. This point is very important inasmuch where a citizen 'found not guilty' and acquitted of his crime by a jury of his peers cannot be the object of future pursuit for the same crime even though evidence against him may come to light at a later date.

IV. Laws and Decisions issued from the Courts
Or Declaration of Duties

The laws and decisions issued from the courts of the land dictate the conduct of a citizen in regards to his duties vis-à-vis the society in which he lives. This is the reason for which we have allowed ourselves to call it a "Declaration of Duties".

Although their decisions have 'force of law', the Supreme Court of the United States, those of the States and other lower courts appointed, do not edict the laws issued from those decisions. However, they do not oppose directly the laws put in force by the Federal Legislature or those of the States, as long as the citizens are disposed to support these laws. The courts only intervene and pronounce judgments in regards to the laws abiding (or not) the Constitution and at the time a citizen or a group of citizens decides to bring the matter before the courts. We will cite three (3) example amongst many which have been considered as 'celebrated causes' issued from decisions made by the Supreme Court of the United States; The Miranda Ruling; Roe versus Wade and the Sullivan Rule.

The Miranda Ruling – Is once again, to be considered as the most celebrated decision made by the Supreme Court of the United States. We have discussed the case earlier in Factor 1 and invite the reader to take another look at the discussion thereof.

The ROE versus WADE Affair

One of the Supreme Court's decisions, which continues to arouse interest, is the ROE versus WADE affair – between the pro and anti abortion camps. In 1970, Norma McCorvey, under the pseudonym of 'Jane Roe', unmarried was pregnant. She and her physician, Dr. Hallford launched a class action suit against the State of Texas, challenging the law which prohibited abortion, except in the case where the mother's life was deemed to be in danger, as evidenced by the family physician. Separately, John and Mary Doe, a childless couple, challenged the same law at about the same time. The decision from the Supreme Court of the United States was handed down on January 22, 1973. It stated formally that the law in question regarding abortion violated the constitutional rights of the plaintiff (and that of all other women in similar circumstances) – under the Ninth and Fourteenth Amendments to the Constitution of the United States. The decision further stated that any woman has the right to interrupt an undesirable pregnancy, even though she could not provide evidence that such pregnancy was endangering her life.

This decision is one of the most controversial in the History of the United States. It opened the door to the creation of two factions which continues to animate the abortion debates since 1973. The debates are in fact, so passionate and the factions so solidly entrenched and influential amid the political arenas that the politicians have a hard time deciding which position to favor. On the one side, we have the religious congregations; the "Pro Life" which is decidedly opposed to the abortion proposal and on the other, we have feminist's organizations or "Pro Choice" which deems it to be a woman's choice to have an abortion or to stay pregnant. This debate has lasted for the past thirty years and there doesn't seem to be any light at the end of the tunnel. Recently, Mrs. Roe, the woman who started it all, threw herself back into the battle. This time, however, she had changed camps and went to the "Pro Life" side – totally opposed to abortion! Was it a reversal of conscience or a last curtsey craving publicity? Can't say…

The Sullivan Rule

My favorite decision issued by the Supreme Court of the United States is the one that gave unlimited protection to the American Press against ruining judicial pursuits from those holding public offices. The decision is known as the "Sullivan Rule" which was issued from the "New York Times versus Sullivan"

The New York Times in its edition on date of March 29, 1960 published an article paid by civil rights' leaders and other important personalities, which denounced the brutality with which the Montgomery Police force had repressed a demonstration led by black students of this city.

Mr. Sullivan, one of the three commissioners elected to public affairs, in charge, amongst other things, of the Police Supervision, estimated that the allegations contained in the article were false and defamatory. And although he was not cited in the article personally, Mr. Sullivan maintained that the term "Police" referred to him personally. Consequently, he claimed damages and interests in the amount of $1,000,000 against the New York Times and the co-authors of the articles. The Montgomery tribunal and the Supreme Court of the State of Alabama decided in Mr. Sullivan's favor. Therefore, the interested parties found themselves in front of the Supreme Court of the United States which reversed the decision handed down by the other courts.

In its decree dated of March 9, 1964, the Supreme Court has given a constitutional applicable standard to its decision which prohibits "A holder of public functions to claim against the Press, any damages or interests for publishing any comments defamatory or false and related to the holder of public functions' conduct, unless the latter could prove 'actual malice' against his person."

The court further stated that the First and Fourteenth Amendments to the Constitution gave to the citizens and to the Press an absolute and unconditional privilege to criticize or make erroneous comments without malice related to the conduct of public or governmental functions' holders in spite of the injuries that such abuse of this right could engender. And that even if there was proof that the journalist knew or was aware in advance that his comments or allegations were erroneous. It is the duty of the person involved to prove that there was malevolent intent on the part of the journalist – and not the contrary, such as was the case in Sullivan versus New York Times. It was in fact demonstrated in a comparison made by the newspaper, that there was some discrepancies between the paid advertisement and the articles published by the paper surrounding the events of that day. Notwithstanding this, and even if the plaintiff could demonstrate actual malice on the part of the journalist, the decree of the Supreme Court prohibits the tribunals and State courts to pronounce judgment in favor of payment of damages and interests against the press to a citizen holder of public office because of critics of his conduct in the carriage of his functions.

The Supreme Court deemed it a privilege for a citizen and for the Press to criticize without prejudice the conduct of holders of public office, which is similar to the protection granted to officials when a citizen attempts civil suit against him for defamation during the carriage of his functions.

Today this 'privilege' enabling the American Press to criticize public figures without prejudice has reached such proportion that the line between the private and public life of a public official is practically inexistent. It is such that one of the first questions asked of a candidate to public office in the United States would be: "Do you have any skeleton in your closet?" If you have anything to hide, you better abstain from running for public office...

There are thousands of laws enacted annually by the federal legislatures, by the State legislatures and the municipalities without taking into account the millions of judgments pronounced by the courts across the United States.

What is evident is that the American citizen, individually or in organized groups, is ready to initiate laws whenever, wherever required – or have recourse to the tribunals when they deem it necessary.

From what we have discussed, we could conclude that the American Judge is very powerful. Judges have almost unlimited powers to interpret the laws and to reverse them when they deem it to be required or vital. And when it comes to the Supreme Court of the United States, the Constitution gives its members the power, without appeal, over the constitutionality of the laws, the acts and judgments handed down by the lower courts. Nominated for life, the nine members of this majestic court are protected by the Constitution against any maneuvers designed to diminish their salaries in order that they become financially dependent of some other concerns with specific or partial interests.

All in all the merit should go to the People who do not spare any effort to keep the Supreme Guardians of the Constitution quite busy indeed.

Factor 14
The essential forms

Surely due to an error, which I will attribute to my poor knowledge of English at the time; when I passed the examination to obtain my Real Estate License from the State of Indiana, to the question; "Are you at least 18 years of age?" I answered "No!"

I was so intent on answering the main questions of the exam that this query regarding my age seemed without importance even superfluous.

However I learned that these "YES" and "NO" had their importance. At the end of the examination, the correction being done on computer, to my great surprise I was handed the results which said approximately this:

Congratulation Mr. Cisse, you have passed your examination to obtain the State of Indiana Real Estate License successfully. But your response regarding your age indicates that you are not 18 years of age yet. The law in the State of Indiana stipulates that you cannot practice the profession of Real Estate Agent if you are not 18 years of age or older.

Although my date of birth had been introduced into the computer records and my birth certificate was proof enough (I thought) that I was over eighteen years of age, I couldn't convince the examiners that the computer had made a mistake!

It took me four months of numerous interventions and correspondence with the State Real Estate Board to finally obtain my Real Estate Agent License. Thus, a small mistake in filling a form can have very disagreeable, if not unexpected consequences. Remember that the forms you fill out in the States are destined to be proof-read by a computer which will only respond to the instructions submitted by laws en-force in the State where the forms are filed. The computer only treats your answers in accordance to the program's logic. It is worth mentioning that in my case the computer was not programmed to verify my age according to my submitted date of birth but by verifying and only 'proof-reading' my answer to the question posed on the form. Therefore, I was considered to be *under* the age of 18 since I had answered "NO" to the question.

You have probably heard the story of the two terrorists who were among the pirates which led to the suicide attack of the World Trade Center in New York on September 11, 2001. In fact, two of the nineteen terrorists introduced a demand to the immigration services in view of obtaining a 'Permanent Student Status' allowing them to register at the local university. And although Mohamed Atta and his friend were plastered on all of the headlines across the United States, their application was accepted a few months after the attack. Why didn't the immigration notice the error? The logical explanation is that since the two terrorists were dead and didn't represent any further threat to the country's security, no one at the FBI (or CIA) bothered to register their name on the computer so that they would appear on the "Most Wanted" list. If that had been done, the computer at the immigration services would have been alerted and the agents in charge of their applications would have halted the process. Consequently, their applications continued its process unhindered until finally reaching the university where these undesirables were to be registered to follow an "aircraft's pilot license course"!

Only States or Federal laws apply to the filling out and to the filing of these forms – therefore you will need to seek legal advice to ensure that all required questionnaires are answered within the legal guidelines of the State (or Federal Bureau) in which they are en-force.

The forms provided in this book are only examples of the type and format of questionnaires which you may encounter; they are issued from two sources – State and Federal.

1. The forms issued from the States

They are dealing with the incorporation or other administrative interventions which manages the activities of a 'non-profit-organization'. The concept and presentation of these forms will most likely vary from State to State – although the information required remains the same. However, you will need to inquire at the Secretary of State's level as to the proper form to use given your particular circumstances.

Note: The examples offered here, are en-force in the State of Indiana only.

2. The forms issued at Federal Levels

They deal with the taxation laws applicable to all organizations across the country. The 'Federal Forms' are similar in all States, Territories and Possessions under Federal jurisdiction. However the treatment centers vary from State to State – you need to inquire where and how the various forms need to be filed.

In any case is it highly recommended to seek legal advice or specialized assistance in order to fill out any of these forms properly – so that you don't become part of the 'statistics' of those who didn't reach their goal because of an error of appreciation or a computer glitch.

As we have discussed in Factor 1, the forms are classified in a chronological order and represent what most organization will need to submit – in the beginning – to determine its standing in the community and its fiscal status.

1. Articles of Incorporation for a Non profit Corporation (State)

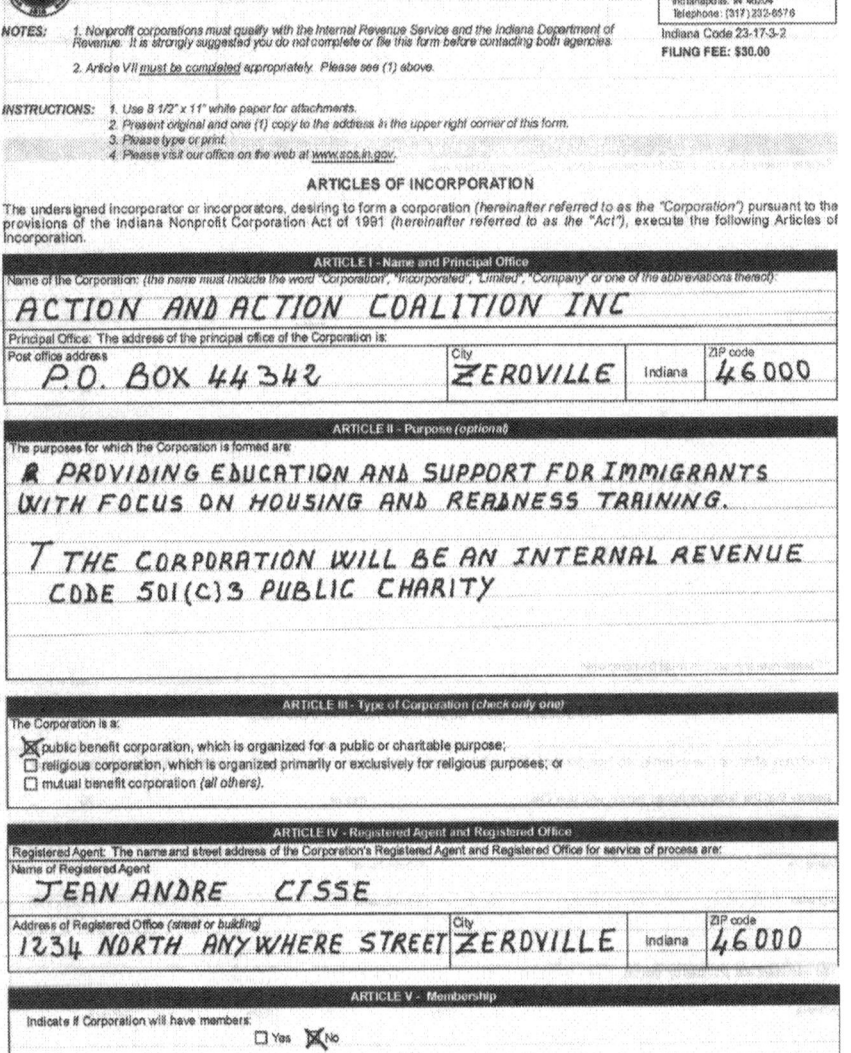

Note: This document comprises two pages; we have reproduced only the first.

2. Application for Employer Identification Number – Form
SS-4 - (federal)

Form **SS-4** (Rev. December 2001) Department of the Treasury Internal Revenue Service	**Application for Employer Identification Number** (For use by employers, corporations, partnerships, trusts, estates, churches, government agencies, Indian tribal entities, certain individuals, and others.) ▶ See separate instructions for each line. ▶ Keep a copy for your records.	EIN OMB No. 1545-0003

Type or print clearly

1 Legal name of entity (or individual) for whom the EIN is being requested
ACTION AND ACTION COALITION, INC

2 Trade name of business (if different from name on line 1)	3 Executor, trustee, "care of" name **JEAN A. CISSE**

4a Mailing address (room, apt., suite no. and street, or P.O. box) **P.O. BOX 44343**	5a Street address (if different) (Do not enter a P.O. box.) **1234 N. ANYWHERE STREET**
4b City, state, and ZIP code **ZEROVILLE IN 46000**	5b City, state, and ZIP code **ZEROVILLE, IN 46000**

6 County and state where principal business is located
MARION

7a Name of principal officer, general partner, grantor, owner, or trustor **JEAN A. CISSE**	7b SSN, ITIN, or EIN **100-00-0000**

8a Type of entity (check only one box)
☐ Sole proprietor (SSN) ____
☐ Partnership
☐ Corporation (enter form number to be filed) ▶ ____
☐ Personal service corp.
☐ Church or church-controlled organization
☒ Other nonprofit organization (specify) ▶ **PUBLIC CHARITY**
☐ Other (specify) ▶

☐ Estate (SSN of decedent) ____
☐ Plan administrator (SSN) ____
☐ Trust (SSN of grantor) ____
☐ National Guard ☐ State/local government
☐ Farmers' cooperative ☐ Federal government/military
☐ REMIC ☐ Indian tribal governments/enterprises
Group Exemption Number (GEN) ▶

8b If a corporation, name the state or foreign country (if applicable) where incorporated | State **INDIANA** | Foreign country

9 Reason for applying (check only one box)
☒ Started new business (specify type) ▶ **PUBLIC CHARITY**
☐ Hired employees (Check the box and see line 12.)
☐ Compliance with IRS withholding regulations
☐ Other (specify) ▶
☐ Banking purpose (specify purpose) ▶ ____
☐ Changed type of organization (specify new type) ▶ ____
☐ Purchased going business
☐ Created a trust (specify type) ▶ ____
☐ Created a pension plan (specify type) ▶ ____

10 Date business started or acquired (month, day, year) **12-25-19--**	11 Closing month of accounting year **DECEMBER**

12 First date wages or annuities were paid or will be paid (month, day, year). Note: *If applicant is a withholding agent, enter date income will first be paid to nonresident alien. (month, day, year)* . . . . ▶

13 Highest number of employees expected in the next 12 months. Note: *If the applicant does not expect to have any employees during the period, enter "-0-."* . . . . ▶	Agricultural	Household	Other

14 Check one box that best describes the principal activity of your business. ☐ Health care & social assistance ☐ Wholesale-agent/broker
☐ Construction ☐ Rental & leasing ☐ Transportation & warehousing ☐ Accommodation & food service ☐ Wholesale-other ☐ Retail
☐ Real estate ☐ Manufacturing ☐ Finance & insurance ☒ Other (specify)

15 Indicate principal line of merchandise sold; specific construction work done; products produced; or services provided.
PROVIDING EDUCATION FOR IMMIGRANT

16a Has the applicant ever applied for an employer identification number for this or any other business? . . . . . ☐ Yes ☒ No
Note: *If "Yes," please complete lines 16b and 16c.*

16b If you checked "Yes" on line 16a, give applicant's legal name and trade name shown on prior application if different from line 1 or 2 above.
Legal name ▶ Trade name ▶

16c Approximate date when, and city and state where, the application was filed. Enter previous employer identification number if known.

Approximate date when filed (mo., day, year)	City and state where filed	Previous EIN

Third Party Designee	Complete this section only if you want to authorize the named individual to receive the entity's EIN and answer questions about the completion of this form.	
	Designee's name **N/A**	Designee's telephone number (include area code) ( )
	Address and ZIP code **N/A**	Designee's fax number (include area code) ( )

Under penalties of perjury, I declare that I have examined this application, and to the best of my knowledge and belief, it is true, correct, and complete.

Name and title (type or print clearly) ▶ **JEAN A. CISSE**	Applicant's telephone number (include area code) **(319) 000-0000**
Signature ▶ *Non Lisible* Date ▶ **12-29-19--**	Applicant's fax number (include area code) **(319) 000-0000**

For Privacy Act and Paperwork Reduction Act Notice, see separate instructions. Cat. No. 16055N Form **SS-4** (Rev. 12-2001)

3. Application for Recognition of Exemption under Section 501(c)3 of the Internal Revenue Code – Form 1023 - (Federal)

Form **1023** (Rev. September 1998) Department of the Treasury Internal Revenue Service	**Application for Recognition of Exemption** **Under Section 501(c)(3) of the Internal Revenue Code**	OMB No. 1545-0056 **Note:** *If exempt status is approved, this application will be open for public inspection*

Read the instructions for each Part carefully.
A User Fee must be attached to this application.
If the required information and appropriate documents are not submitted along with Form 8718 (with payment of the appropriate user fee), the application may be returned to you.
Complete the Procedural Checklist on page 8 of the instructions.

Part I   Identification of Applicant

1a Full name of organization (as shown in organizing document) *ACTION & ACTION COALITIO Inc*	2 Employer identification number (EIN) (If none, see page 3 of the Specific Instructions.) *35 00000*
1b c/o Name (if applicable)	3 Name and telephone number of person to be contacted if additional information is needed
1c Address (number and street) Room/Suite *123 N. ANYWHERE STREET*	*(317) 000 - 0000*
1d City, town, or post office, state, and ZIP + 4. If you have a foreign address, see **Specific Instructions** for Part I, page 3. *ZEROVILLE IN 46000*	4 Month the annual accounting period ends *DECEMBER*
1e Web site address	5 Date incorporated or formed *12-25-1900* 6 Check here if applying under section: a ☐ 501(e) b ☐ 501(f) c ☐ 501(k) d ☐ 501(n)

7	Did the organization previously apply for recognition of exemption under this Code section or under any other section of the Code? . . . . ☐ Yes ☒ No If "Yes," attach an explanation.
8	Is the organization required to file Form 990 (or Form 990-EZ)? . . . . ☐ N/A ☒ Yes ☐ No If "No," attach an explanation (see page 3 of the **Specific Instructions**).
9	Has the organization filed Federal income tax returns or exempt organization information returns? . . ☐ Yes ☒ No If "Yes," state the form numbers, years filed, and Internal Revenue office where filed.

10	Check the box for the type of organization. ATTACH A CONFORMED COPY OF THE CORRESPONDING ORGANIZING DOCUMENTS TO THE APPLICATION BEFORE MAILING. (See **Specific Instructions** for Part I, Line 10, on page 3.) See also Pub. 557 for examples of organizational documents.)
	a ☒ Corporation— Attach a copy of the Articles of Incorporation (including amendments and restatements) showing approval by the appropriate state official; also include a copy of the bylaws.
	b ☐ Trust— Attach a copy of the Trust Indenture or Agreement, including all appropriate signatures and dates.
	c ☐ Association— Attach a copy of the Articles of Association, Constitution, or other creating document, with a declaration (see instructions) or other evidence the organization was formed by adoption of the document by more than one person; also include a copy of the bylaws.

If the organization is a corporation or an unincorporated association that has not yet adopted bylaws, check here ▶ ☐

I declare under the penalties of perjury that I am authorized to sign this application on behalf of the above organization and that I have examined this application, including the accompanying schedules and attachments, and to the best of my knowledge it is true, correct and complete.

Please Sign Here ▶	*Nonlsubla* (Signature)	*JEAN A. CISSE* (Type or print name and title or authority of signer)	*12-10-19.-* (Date)

For Paperwork Reduction Act Notice, see page 7 of the instructions.   Cat. No. 17133K

Note: This document contains approximately ten pages; we have only reproduced the first one.

Moussa Cissé

4. Application for Certificate of Authority of a Foreign Corporation (to transact Business in the State of ...)

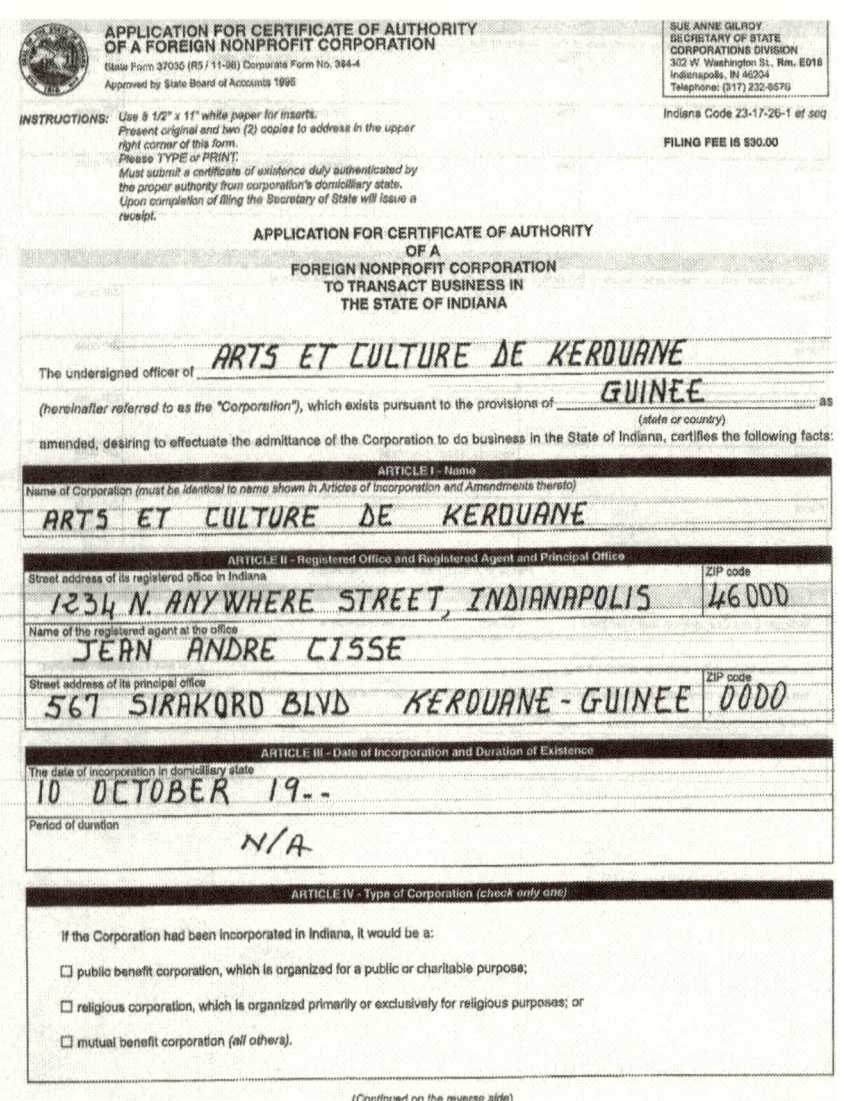

Note: This document is to be used solely by organizations incorporated in one of the States of United States and which may be desirous to do business in another State. It comprises two pages and we have only reproduced the first one.

5. Certificate of Assumed Business Name (all Entities) optional (State)

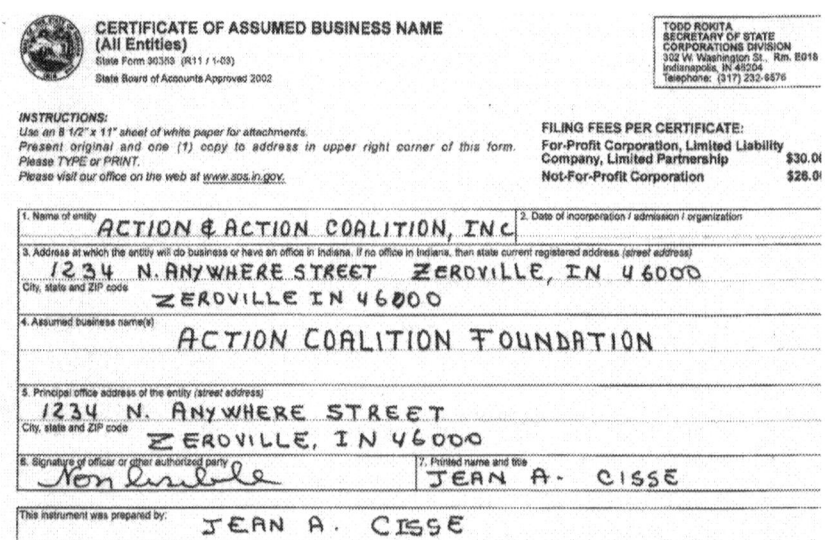

Note: This step is optional. Nevertheless, the laws in most States demand that the legal name of an incorporated entity makes mention of either of the following terms: 'Corporation', 'Incorporated', 'Limited', 'Company' or an abbreviated version thereof.

Example: *"Action and Action Coalition Incorporated"* or the abbreviated version: *"Action and Action Coalition Inc."*

If you feel, for some reason, that using the full name of your organization is somewhat cumbersome or difficult to remember, you may choose to use an alias when filling out this form.

Example: *"Action and Action Coalition Incorporated"* could use the alias: *"Action and Action Coalition"*; or *"Action Coalition Network."*

However, the legal name of your organization needs to be used in all legal or official report made to the government (i.e. Tax Returns). Some forms or reports will demand that you mention both names when filling out their questionnaires.

The legal name of *"United States African Housing Foundation"* is *"United States African Housing Corporation"* which the directors chose not to use in view of the fact that many of our partners thought of our organization as one of commercial endeavors (and not one 'not-for-profit').

6. Indiana Business Entity Report (State)

INDIANA BUSINESS ENTITY REPORT
State Form 48725 (R2 / 1-03)
Approved by State Board of Accounts, 1998
Prescribed by Todd Rokita, Secretary of State

INSTRUCTIONS:
1. Complete sections A-H. (Section H is located on the back of the form.)
2. Make check payable to the Indiana Secretary of State.
3. Mail form and check to P.O. Box 7087, Indianapolis, IN 46207

PRESORTED
FIRST CLASS MAIL
U.S. POSTAGE PAID
INDIANAPOLIS, IN
PERMIT NO. 2682

A. All entity types must complete this section.

Current entity name and principal office address | Please make any changes to address here

ACTION AND ACTION COALITION, Inc

1234 N ANYWHERE STREET
INDIANAPOLIS IN 46000

B. All entity types must complete this section.

Current filing year: 1900 | Past filing years reported on this form: 1800

C. All entity types must complete this section.

Date of Incorporation / Qualification / Formation | Domicile State

D. All entity types must complete this section. Please check the appropriate type for your corporate entity.

☐ Business Corporation ☐ Professional Corporation ☒ Non profit Corporation ☐ Ag Coop ☐ Limited Liability Company

E. All entity types must complete this section. A P.O. box is not an acceptable address unless accompanied by a rural route number.

Current registered agent and registered address | Please make changes to agent and address here.

JEAN A. CISSE
1234 N ANYWHERE STREET
INDIANAPOLIS IN 46000

N/A

F. All entity types except LLCs complete this section.

Current President or highest officer and address | Please make changes to officer and address here.

MAMADOU SYLLA
548 WEST ANYTIME AVENUE
ZEROVILLE IN 46000

N/A

Current Secretary or other officer and address | Please make changes to officer and address here.

OUMAR KABA
4981 SOUTH NOWHERE ROAD
ZEROVILLE IN 4600

N/A

G. Must be signed by a corporate officer, chairman of the board or by a member or manager of an LLC.

Non SIGN HERE

This document is signed under the penalties of perjury.
(If fee is blank, check the fee schedule on back.)
TOTAL FEES DUE:

Note: This annual report is mandatory for all entities. It is addressed to the Secretary of State. Its aim is to keep up-to-date the vital information concerning your organization such as name and address of person (or persons) responsible for its management and direction. This report is not to be confused with the Annual Tax Return which was not pertinent to be given in example in this publication.

www.ingramcontent.com/pod-product-compliance
Lightning Source LLC
Chambersburg PA
CBHW030314290526
45785CB00001B/346